Stepping ꓢtones to Creativity

by Judith Harries, Mel Astill and Elizabeth Palfrey

Contents

WITHDRAWN

Published by Practical Pre-School Books,
A Division of MA Education Ltd, St Jude's Church,
Dulwich Road, Herne Hill, London, SE24 0PB

Tel: 020 7738 5454 www.practicalpreschoolbooks.com

© MA Education Ltd 2009

Illustrations by Cathy Hughes. Front cover images clockwise from top left © iStockphoto/Jean Schweitzer, iStockphoto/Soubrette,

Dreamstime.com/Karen Struthers. Back cover image from left to right © iStockphoto/Jaimie Duplass, iStockphoto/Jan Tyler, Dreamstime.com/Glenda Powers, iStockphoto/Gary Sludden

ISBN 978-1-907241-00-0

What is creativity?

Stepping Stones to Creativity is a series of books that aim to provide early years practitioners with a treasure trove of practical activities and resources to help develop the budding creativity of children in their care. Each book focuses on a different area of creativity, which is explored through forty of the most popular early years topics. In each topic you will find activities that support the five Early Learning Goals of Creative Development, so that you can ensure you are meeting the requirements of the Early Years Foundation Stage.

Many of these activities can be adapted for even younger children or extended to benefit Key Stage One children.

Creativity In The Classroom

Creativity is an elusive term. Although great enjoyment can be taken from working with imaginative children in the Early Years who are naturally eager to explore, in practice there are some key issues which face the practitioner:

What is 'creativity'?
In a nutshell, it is the ability to use knowledge and skills, plus a healthy dollop of imagination, to tackle and solve any problem. It is about taking risks and being involved in the learning process. Creative thinking does not just apply to obviously 'creative' tasks such as art or music, but can be used in investigations in science and across the foundation stage curriculum. To develop creativity children need time, space, and multiple opportunities to experiment with materials and ideas. They also need to be encouraged to make connections between ideas as they play.

How can we as practitioners make this happen for the children in our care?
Young children are curious by nature. They learn by exploring and experimenting and 'having a go'. As practitioners we need to provide a stimulating environment together with lots of opportunities and of course unlimited time! Although it can be a challenge in multi-purpose buildings, a creative environment can be created by leaving art materials and musical instruments out for children to play and experiment with.

Does there always need to be an 'end product' to creativity?
Practitioners and parents often both fall into the trap of only valuing an 'end product' as proof of creativity. How many of us have heard an anxious parent berating their young child with the words, 'have you made me a painting this morning Tom?' Children sometimes learn to rush to the painting easel and apply a few hurried strokes of paint to appease their carer, even though they may have been involved all morning playing imaginatively and creatively in the role-play area. We need to appreciate creative play and processes as just as important as any finished artwork!

What is the value of creative group work?
In many settings, children often work together to produce joint artwork and models, as well as singing, drama, dance and music performances. This can be seemingly problematic, as at times the individual creative process may have to be subordinated to the purpose and will of the group. However, group creative work can provide an ideal opportunity to develop children's social and co-operative skills. More often than not it requires more imagination and creativity to work as a group!

What can practitioners do to develop children's creativity?
You may now be feeling how do I encourage children in my care to develop their creativity? The following are useful hints for nurturing young children's creativity:

- Provide sufficient time and opportunities for children to explore, experiment and practice their skills. Allow children time to work at their own speed. Try to avoid them being pressured by other children eager to try another activity.
- Some children require more encouragement to 'have a go' on their own. They may need you to suggest ideas, stimulate their imagination, and encourage them. Children will discover a lot through their own explorations, but unless there is an adult on hand to talk about their discoveries, learning opportunities can be missed.
- Children need to feel secure. They need to know that help is available if and when they need it. The tricky job is judging when to intervene if a child is struggling. Sometimes the process of problem-solving is part of the learning process, but do be prepared to model and teach new skills that children may require in order to progress. Experience will help you maintain the balance between being intrusive, and avoiding the frustration children feel when their own efforts are thwarted.
- Supply good quality resources – both materials and people! Challenge children by inviting artists or performers to show children their own particular area of creativity. In particular make use of talented parents who are willing to help.
- Encourage children to talk to each other about their work. Ask them to share how they overcame problems when constructing a model robot, or why they decided to make a loud sound at the end of the music.
- Try to be creative yourself! How long is it since you found time to develop your own creative gifts? Challenge yourself to learn a new skill this year.

Creativity and the EYFS

Creative development is one of the six areas of learning in the Early Years Foundation Stage – the curriculum for all children under the age of five. The Statutory Framework, published in 2007, breaks down Creative Development into the four following aspects.

The Four Aspects of Creative Development:

Being Creative – Responding to Experiences, Expressing and Communicating Ideas

Corresponding E.L.G.: Respond in a variety of ways to what they see, hear, smell, touch or feel.

Corresponding E.L.G.: Express and communicate their ideas, thoughts and feelings by using a widening range of materials, suitable tools, imaginative and role-play, movement, designing and making, and a variety of songs and musical instruments.

Exploring Media and Materials

Corresponding E.L.G.: Explore colour, texture, shape, form and space in two and three dimensions.

Creating Music and Dance

Corresponding E.L.G.: Recognise and explore how sounds can be changed, sing simple songs from memory, recognise repeated sounds and sound patterns and match movements to music.

Developing Imagination and Imaginative Play

Corresponding E.L.G.: Use their imagination in art and design, music, dance, imaginative and role-play and stories.

Using this book

All forty topics in this book include suggestions for activities that explore four different areas of creativity: drama and role-play; stories, songs and rhymes; design, art and modelling; and dance and movement.

The following sections detail how to make the most of each area, and detail the importance of each set of skills to the Early Years Foundation Stage.

Drama and Role-Play

Interestingly, the actual word 'drama' is not included in the Early Learning Goals for Creative Development but it clearly underlies a great deal of the goals' intentions.

A child is surely 'being creative' when, through drama and role-play, they are able to show a personal response to a dramatic, if pretend, situation. Drama games and skills enable children to 'express and communicate' their own ideas in a fun, imaginative and creative way. In an increasingly technological world children are spoonfed acceptable responses through exposure to passive entertainment in the form of television programmes and computer games. The world of drama and role-play can provide a vital medium for the development of imagination and imaginative play.

All practitioners desire to extend children's creativity by supporting their natural curiosity through play and exploration. Role-play areas should be inspirational, open-ended environments that enable children's creative learning, encouraging them to feel safe and secure as they extend their experiences of life. These environments offer many opportunities to develop cross-curricular learning, in particular language development, awareness of a variety of cultures, and knowledge and understanding of the world around us.

Using the drama activities in this book

Drama games

These games are great as starting points for a drama session, or to introduce a new topic to your children in a creative way. Many of them are fun 'warm-up' games that help the children to relax and feel comfortable with each other so that they are confident and able to express themselves in a non-threatening environment. These may be thinking word games, informal circle games, or energetic physical activities, which require more space and warm up bodies as well as minds.

Mime

The skills of mime require a great deal of concentration and these focused activities will develop children's ability to use their imagination and their bodies to tell stories and describe thoughts and feelings. Many of the games and activities can be adapted for use in other topics, for instance the game Mirrors works well across the topics of 'Food', 'Clothes' and 'Ourselves'.

Drama skills

This is the most varied section, which includes the development of some specific dramatic skills such as 'freeze frames', 'hot-seating',

Using this book

retelling stories, changing the endings of stories, and character studies. This section is called 'Drama skills' as the activities involved often extend a skill learned earlier in a drama game or mime activity. There are lots of suggestions for improvised dramas, which take the children beyond pretend play into stories with characters, dilemmas and crucially, resolutions. These are most effective if the teacher is prepared to go 'in role' and join in the drama to sensitively direct where necessary.

Role-play

Each topic is also matched to a suitable role-play scenario that can be set up simply in most settings. Instructions are included for the equipment required, as well as ideas for making homemade features. Possible roles that the children might like to explore are listed, along with lots of ideas for stories to be acted out, with or without teacher input.

Stories, Songs and Rhymes

Stories

Stories can be used as a tool for creative development by providing a stimulus for work in all sorts of media. Hearing and using the language of stories also encourages children to use that language in their role-play.

Using the stories in this book

This book suggests a wealth of stories to read with children in the early years, these vary from traditional tales to modern picture books and even original stories, written especially for this book. Each story comes with a suggested creative activity designed to allow children to explore elements of the story further. Each of these activities is linked with one of the four aspects of Creative Development.

Songs

Singing is one of the earliest forms of creative expression and children are exposed to it even before they are born. Many mothers instinctively croon to their unborn child or small baby. As children develop language they will begin to express themselves vocally and through song. Singing in a group is at the beginning of musical life for all of us. The songs in this book are easy to learn as the majority are set to well-known tunes from nursery rhymes or traditional songs. The few original songs featured in this book are provided with notation in case you are feeling brave.

Rhymes

Recognising rhyme is a crucial part of developing creative listening skills, leading to an understanding of the patterns involved in words and music. The use of rhyme clearly overlaps with the Early Learning Goals for Communication, Language and Literacy, as learning songs and rhymes from memory is a vital part of learning to read. The rhymes in this book vary between finger and action rhymes through to poems and even raps.

Using the songs and rhymes in this book

Each song or rhyme in this book offers various possibilities for children to further develop their creative abilities. There are traditional songs and rhymes, variations on these, as well as brand new songs and rhymes.

In order to encourage as much creative play as possible, below are some suggestions for adapting each song or rhyme. At first these are likely to be led by the practitioner, but as children become used to experimenting with songs, rhythm and movement they will become confident in making up their own versions.

- Enjoy suggesting simple actions for children to copy and encourage children to create their own movements.
- Encourage movement to the rhythm and 'marching out' the beat.
- Suggest variations to the verse and ask children to come up with their own alternatives. For example "What are you wearing today/My coat and hat, coat and hat", "What are you wearing today/My scarf and gloves, scarf and gloves".

There are of course many other uses for the wealth of stories, songs and rhymes contained within this book, and it is hoped that the design of the book will allow each practitioner to adapt these to their individual teaching style.

Design, Art and Modelling

Activities in each topic are divided into the following areas:

Pencils and pens

These include opportunities, from simple mark making and sketching arrangements of still life, to wax crayon rubbings, drawings of the inner workings of machines and chalk playground games.

Useful resources: different thicknesses of pencils, crayons, gel and felt pens, wax crayons, chalks, pastels, charcoal, etc.

Paint and print

Painting activities range from representational painting, such as self-portraits, to more abstract ideas using shapes and colours.

Using this book

Ideas cover finger painting, using different sized brushes, textured paint and printing with non-traditional objects to create a variety of effects.

Useful resources: powder paint, ready mix, acrylic and water colour paints, inks, paint brushes, feathers, string, toothbrushes, sponges, natural and found objects, etc.

Collage
This could be re-entitled 'materials' as the activities use a huge variety of different materials to create collage effects of planets, bears, pirate ships and more abstract patterns.

Useful resources: different types of paper, card, plastic, aluminum foil, bubble wrap, fabric, sequins, beads, buttons, straws, pasta, sticks, string, wool, natural materials, etc.

Modelling
Create 2D or 3D models, ranging from sock puppets to dream catchers.

Useful resources: pipe cleaners, straws, balloons, papers, card, modroc, newspaper, junk, wood, fabric, wool, etc.

Clay and dough
Experiment with different types of malleable materials and create a wealth of finished products, such as clay candlesticks and hedgehogs, salt and flour dough mobiles, and playdough food.

Useful resources: homemade or commercial playdough, plasticine, salt and flour dough, air dry or kiln fired clay, etc. See p.19 for a recipe for playdough.

Famous Art
Opportunities to introduce young children to many different famous artists and works of art from Renoir to Picasso and Dali to the animation of Walt Disney.

Some useful websites for finding art to use in your classroom:
www.wga.hu (web gallery of art),
www.moma.org (Museum of Modern Art),
www.famousartistgallery.com,
www.didgeswedoo.com.

Dance and Movement

Dance and movement are referred to throughout the aspects of Creative Development and the importance of providing children with opportunities for both are frequently mentioned within the effective practice guidance of the EYFS. Through dance and movement children are able to express their imagination and creativity free from the fear of failure, as there is no right or wrong way to dance. Dance is a medium that enables children to build confidence in their own abilities as it continuously offers a sense of achievement. Children can respond to experiences in their own unique manner, working either individually or with others, all the while developing their ideas and creative approach.

Warm Up
These short sessions are designed to introduce topics to children whilst at the same time limbering them up in preparation for physical exercise. The warm up should be a time for children to become at ease within the group, as they need to feel secure and relaxed in order to have the confidence to express themselves freely. Children should feel comfortable in conveying their own interpretations of each idea.

Dance
Each topic has suggestions for dance. Some dance is set to music, whilst others can be performed to well-known rhymes or songs. Many of the dances incorporate media and materials to enhance the experiences. These props can further develop creativity as children begin to explore and understand colours, textures, forms and space. Teacher input is a great way to encourage movement but be careful not to over demonstrate aims and intentions, as this may limit children's own thoughts and expression.

Movement Games
Games are linked to the topics and provide time for the group to play together imaginatively, often involving role play and some use of props. Almost all can be played both indoors or outdoors, adding further learning opportunities and additional dimensions.

Cool Down
It is critical that children have sufficient time to relax after physical play, and this is exactly the aim of each cool down. These activities should be conducted in a calm environment away from distractions wherever possible, ensuring appropriate room temperatures are maintained with adequate ventilation and access to fresh drinking water.

Animals

Drama and Role Play

Drama games

- Sit in a circle and pass round animal sounds: hissing, roaring, squeaking, mooing, and so on. Try not to repeat a previous sound.
- *Noah's Ark:* Make a collection of cards showing matching pairs of animals and hand them out to children. Ask the children to move around the room making the sounds and actions for their animal and try to find their partner to go into the ark.

Mimes

- *Animal antics:* In the style of the game 'beans' invite children to mime different animals. Call out 'cheetah' and ask the children to run fast around the room on all fours. Try 'snake' – sliding along floor; 'rabbit' – bunny hops; 'elephant' – move slowly, swinging a trunk; 'parrot' – fly around the room; 'crocodile' – snapping jaws, and 'horse' – children find a partner and trot around like a pantomime horse! Can the children think up some more animal mimes of their own?

Drama skills

- Use animal puppets to help children make up stories about animals from traditional tales or picture books.
- *Visit to the zoo:* Improvise a family trip to the zoo. Introduce the characters in the family. Talk about the preparation for the trip and the journey. At the zoo set up some situations or problems for the children to face in the drama such as: an escaped lion, the zookeeper needs help feeding the penguins, or one of the animals is sick.

Role-play

The vet's surgery

Set up: A waiting room with reception area, telephone, diary, computer-screen, posters, leaflets, pet food, chairs, a consulting room with table, scales, medical kit, soft toy animals and carrying boxes or baskets.

Roles: Vet, nurse, pet owners, receptionist, animals.

Stories: Cat escapes in the waiting room; poorly new pet; animal won't keep still to be examined; animal is too big to fit in the room (e.g. a horse or kangaroo); vet is scared of snakes! Read and act out the story *Mog and the V.E.T.* by Judith Kerr.

Stories, Songs and Rhymes

Stories

 The Gruffalo by Julia Donaldson
Design your own scary monster masks.

 Rumble in the Jungle by Giles Andreae
Enjoy reciting poems and adding animal sound effects.

 Noah's Ark Traditional
Give each child a partner and create a dance of pairs of animals going on and off the ark.

 The Leopard's Drum by Jessica Souhami
Act out the story, moving like the different animals from the story.

Walking through the jungle
What do I feel?
I can feel spider webs silvery and real.

I'm A Stripey Tiger
(Tune: I'm A Little Teapot)
I'm a stripey tiger, orange and black
See my stripes go down my back.
When I'm in the jungle, hear me roar
Then I sleep and start to snore!

Design, Art and Modelling

Pencils and pens

- *Animal autographs:* Draw and sketch favourite animals from photographs using soft pencils and/or charcoal. Ask children not to forget to sign their pictures!

Paint and print

- *Animal prints:* Look at pictures of different animal skin prints such as zebra, tiger, cow and giraffe. Paint versions of them using pale coloured sugar paper and brown and black paint.
- *Big cat diary:* Provide large outline shapes or templates of tigers and leopards and invite children to print on patterns using strips of corrugated cardboard for stripes or lids of felt tip pens for spots. Can they think of a way to turn the cats into lions?

Collage

- *Who am I?:* Talk about different types of animal covering, such as skin, fur, scales, feathers and spines. Use collage materials to create fantasy animals with a variety of coats. Ask children to think of a funny name for each animal. This will make a great display.

Modelling

- *Animal masks:* Use simple pre-cut cardboard mask shapes, (see templates at the back of this book) and help children to cut out the eye holes. Provide a variety of noses, ears and whiskers such as rabbit, mouse, cat, elephant, monkey, etc. Paint the masks and attach elastic.
- *Bottle-top rattle snake:* Under supervision let children hammer holes in lots of metal bottle tops and thread on to a shoe lace or length of string. Choose a bead for the head.

Songs and rhymes

- Old Macdonald Had A Farm
- I Went To The Animal Fair
- Who Built The Ark?
- Baa Baa Black Sheep
- One Grey Elephant Balancing
- An Elephant Goes Like This And That
- The Animals Went In Two By Two
- Daddy's Taking Me To The Zoo Tomorrow
- The Lion And The Unicorn

Old Macdonald Had A Zoo
(Tune: Old Macdonald Had A Farm)
Old MacDonald had a zoo
E I E I O
And in that zoo there was a lion
E I E I O
With a roar, roar here
And a roar, roar there
Here a roar, there a roar
Everywhere a roar, roar,
Old MacDonald had a zoo
E I E I O
What animals would you find in Old MacDonald's safari park/ petshop/pond/lake etc.?

Walking Through The Jungle
Walking through the jungle
What do I see?
I can see a tiger looking at me.
Walking through the jungle
What do I hear?
I can hear a parrot squawk very near.

Clay and dough

- *Clay hedgehogs:* Use dough or clay to sculpt 3D model animals. Make hedgehogs by adding cut up straws to a ball of clay. Can the children think of other animals they could make?

Famous Art

Henri Rousseau – Jungle Sunset & Tropical Rainforest with Monkeys

Junglescape: Talk about the animals and landscape in both paintings. Make individual drawings or find pictures of monkeys, lions, toucans, and other jungle creatures. Make a large jungle collage using cut and torn paper in a variety of colours and textures. Ask children to bring their jungle creatures to the collage and stick them into the picture. Will they hide behind the foliage or will they soar above the trees?

Dance and Movement

Warm Up

Who am I?
Children take it in turns to perform animal impressions with sounds e.g. a laughing hyena, a snapping crocodile, a howling monkey or a roaring lion.

Dance

Play Camille Saint-Saens "Les Carnival Des Animaux".

The music reflects the following animals;
- Lions
- Tortoise
- Elephants
- The aquarium
- Donkey
- Fossils

Encourage the children to listen to the music as they move about. How does the music remind them of the animal it represents and how can they move like the animal?

Movement Games

Musical Animals
Play some of the children's favourite music and invite them to dance about however they choose. Explain that when the music is stopped a picture of an animal will be held up and the children can stop dancing and start performing like the

animal being shown. As the children's confidence grows stop the music frequently and provide a wider range of animals for them to impersonate.

Cat & Mouse
Music is played and the children squeak and move around the room like mice. When the music is stopped the mice must remain perfectly still. Any mouse moving is immediately caught by the cat – an adult or child chosen beforehand.

Cool Down

Sleeping lions
Children pretend to be lions settling down for an afternoon nap in the cool shade of a big tree. Once asleep they must remain perfectly still. Any lion caught moving is out. Try to catch the lions out by making them laugh or smile, wriggle or fidget!

Autumn

Drama games

- *Firework display:* Sit in a circle and pass firework sounds around the circle. Try not to repeat any words or sounds. Then add body actions and sounds and perform a firework display.
- *Vegetable soup:* In the style of 'fruit salad' stand in a circle and give each child the name of a vegetable such as carrots, parsnips and pumpkins. Call out a vegetable and those children must change places in the circle. When you call out 'vegetable soup' everyone has to change places!

Mimes

- Mime making soup. Go through the process stage by stage – washing and chopping vegetables, cooking, blending, eating.
- Divide the children into two groups. Ask one group to make the shapes of trees, gently swaying in the wind. As the wind gets stronger the leaves begin to fall (fingers fluttering down to the ground) and acorns and conkers drop off the trees (fists bang on the floor). The other group are the quick squirrels and spiky hedgehogs who are searching for food.

Drama skills

- *The bonfire party:* Improvise a drama at a bonfire party. Talk about the characters who might be at the party. Plan and prepare the food. Build the bonfire. Discuss fireworks and the firework code. Carefully pretend to set off the fireworks. Use some of the children's firework sounds and actions from the firework display game. Carefully introduce some possible problems to the drama such as a scared pet or an injury.

Role-play

Autumn glade

Set up: Simple home corner surrounded by tall trees made from corrugated cardboard trunks. Lots of real autumn leaves strewn about on top of a mat with a scattering of conkers, acorns, and other autumn treasures. Soft toy squirrels, owls, rabbits, mice, hedgehogs etc.

Roles: A family to live in the house, woodland animals etc.

Stories: An Autumn walk; hiding and finding Autumn treasures or food; listening to the sound of scrunching leaves; making a wish when catching a falling leaf; finding and caring for an injured animal. Act out the story of *Pumpkin Soup* by Helen Cooper.

Stories

Autumn Is For Apples by Michelle Knudsen
Use Modroc and newspaper to create model apples. Paint them different shades of yellow, green and red.

Autumn by Gerda Muller
Make plum jam or apple crumble and share at snacktime.

Squirrel Nutkin by Beatrix Potter
Act out the story and learn the cheeky rhymes that Squirrel Nutkin sings to old Mr Brown.

Pumpkin Soup by Helen Cooper
Act out the story as the animals make the soup together, fall out, and then make friends again. Try making some pumpkin soup and carve a pumpkin lantern for Halloween.

Songs and rhymes

- Rolypoly Pudding And Blackberry Pie
- Five Little Leaves So Bright And Gay
- Here Is The Tree With Leaves So Green

Can You Catch a Red One?
(Tune: I Can Sing A Rainbow)
Red and orange and yellow and brown,
All the leaves falling around.
Can you catch a red one,
Catch a red one,
Catch a red one now?

(Then change colours…)

Firework Fingers

Five thin rockets standing tall
Leaning against the garden wall
One went pop
One went bang
One went fizz
One went clang
One went nowhere
And that left none at all.
(Countdown with fingers)

Autumn Memories

Apple peel and pumpkin pie
Golden leaves floating by
Blustery winds and bonfire burning
Prickly conker cases turning
Spiders spin, ghosts grin
Fireworks flash, raindrops splash
Misty Autumn morning here.

Design, Art and Modelling

Pencils and pens

- *Leaf rubbing:* Go for a walk with the children and collect some Autumn leaves. Take a fallen leaf and place it so that the veins face upwards on a piece of paper. Place a second piece of paper on top and rub gently over the leaf shape with a wax crayon held on its side. Repeat with different-sized leaves and use lots of Autumnal colours.

Paint and print

- *Conker rolling:* Line a round shallow metal tray with a circle of paper. Invite children to drop 3 or 4 conkers into different coloured paint. One at a time, spoon the conkers into the tray and roll them gently round watching the paint trail as it emerges.
- *Leaf printing:* Carefully paint the underside of a leaf using Autumnal colours such as yellow, orange, red or brown. Turn the leaf over and place it paint side down on the paper. Place another piece of paper on top and press over the leaf shape with a roller. Lift carefully and repeat until all the paint has been used.

Collage

- *Half leaves:* Prepare a variety of leaf shapes and/or templates. Fold the leaves in half and glue one half down onto paper so that the leaves seem to be falling. Create a swirling display of falling autumn leaves in copper, brown, russet and orange!

Modelling

- *Autumn signs:* Gather together a selection of Autumn materials such as leaves, conkers and their cases, acorns, pine-cones, moss, sticks, feathers, seeds, and so on.

Invite children to arrange them on a block of wood or driftwood and attach using glue or hammer and nails.

Clay and dough

- *Clay pressed leaves:* Roll out the clay to about 5mm thick. Press a leaf onto the clay with the veins side down. Cut around the leaf shape and peel off leaving the impression in the clay. Leave to dry and paint using Autumnal colours.

Famous Art

Gustav Klimt – Birch Forest

Pastel Autumn: Using Autumnal colours and exploring different ways to use the pastels, create a copy of this forest scene. Try using the tip of the pastel for simple lines or lengthways for trunks. Experiment with dots, dashes and smudges until the birch forest is complete!

Dance and Movement

Warm Up

Autumn trees

Imagine you are a tree standing tall with branches out wide. What type of tree are you? What animals live in you? Gently sway about in the breeze. Maybe a strong storm is coming? Encourage the children to shake their branches to loose their leaves.

Dance

Dingle Dangle Scarecrow

Children love to perform this lively action song.

Vivaldi's L'Autumno

You will need a copy of Vivaldi's classic, "The Four Seasons". "L'Autumno" (Autumn) aims to represent the happiness the season brings with everybody being made to forget their cares and to sing and dance as they celebrate the pleasure of a bountiful harvest. As you listen to the music encourage dance that reflects celebration.

Five Fireworks

Stand five children in a row on a bench or a step – somewhere safe for them to jump off into the night sky!

Say the following rhyme:
Five fire works standing in a row
(Children stand with arms above heads pointed like a rocket)
Looking for adventure

Ready to go
5, 4,3,2,1 blast off
WOOOSH away one goes
(One child jumps from the bench and flies into the night sky)
Four fire works...........and so on.

Movement Games

Hot potato

Sitting in a circle give the children a potato (a bean bag will do just as well). As music is played the potato is passed from child to child around the circle. When the music stops the child holding the potato must lie down on the floor where they were sitting. The winner is the last child sitting up.

Cool Down

The Mendi Tree

This is a traditional Indian story for Hindu weddings and celebrations and is intended to be acted out in pairs.

Take red and gold of the morning skies from the leaves of the Mendi Tree *(Reach up pretending to take the leaves)*

Make patterns from these special dyes *(Mime stirring the leaves into a paste)*

On the hands of you and me *(Point to your partner and then yourself)*

Take little hands, and decorate *(Hold hands out to your partner)*

With mango, leaves, and curls *(Take turns to draw patterns using fingers on each others hands)*

A paisley pattern of your own with Mendi shapes and swirls *(Hold partners hand and turn slowly)*

Bears

Drama games

- *Share-a-bear:* Sit in a circle and pass a special 'shared bear' around. Encourage children to feel that when holding the bear they can share some happy or sad news with the group.
- *Bear Hugs:* Ask children to bring in bears from home. Move around the room with their bears as you shake a tambourine. When you tap it they must 'hug' the nearest bear and its owner, very tight!

Mime

- *Sleepy Bear's Honey Pot:* Sit in a circle and invite one child to be Sleepy Bear in the middle with a small pot placed behind him or her. Point at another child to creep into the circle and take the pot without waking Sleepy Bear. Make it more difficult by putting something in the pot that makes a sound when moved!
- *Bears:* Play this mime game in the style of 'beans'. Start by introducing two or three different bears such as 'Black Bear' – rear up on hind legs and growl, 'Brown Bear' – curl up and hibernate and 'Polar Bear' – slide around on all fours. Later add 'Spectacled Bear' – make glasses using hands, and 'Teddy Bear' – hug the nearest person.

Drama skills

- *We're All Going On A Bear Hunt:* Act out the well-known rhyme by Michael Rosen.
- Talk about the three bears from the story of Goldilocks. Practise using voices in different ways to represent the three bears: Daddy Bear's low growly voice, Mummy Bear's middle normal voice, Baby Bear's high squeaky voice. Play who's coming to breakfast? Ask the question together and take turns to reply using one of the bear's voices. Can the children guess which bear is coming to breakfast?
- Help children to act out the scene from Goldilocks when the three bears return to the house to find there has been an intruder! Interview characters from the story including Goldilocks. Make up a new ending and act it out.

Role-play

Three Bear's House

Set up: Three different sized bowls, chairs and beds, bear masks or dressing-up suits, other home furniture.

Roles: Goldilocks, three bears, other traditional story characters who could visit the house such as Jack, the big bad wolf, Hansel and Gretel, Little Red Riding Hood.

Stories: Mix and match Goldilocks with other fairy tales.

Stories

 We're Going on a Bear Hunt by Michael Rosen
Chant the words of the rhyme and add actions and sound effects using musical instruments.

 Goldilocks and the Three Bears Traditional
Act out the story. What happens when the three bears return to the house and find the intruder?

 This Is The Bear by Sarah Hayes
Make annotated posters of Bear's adventures.

 Where's My Teddy? by Jez Alborough
Draw spot the teddy pictures using ICT.

Songs and rhymes

- When Goldilocks Went To The House Of The Bears
- The Bear Went Over The Mountain
- Teddy Bear, Teddy Bear, Touch Your Nose
- The Teddy Bears' Picnic
- Round And Round The Garden Like A Teddy Bear

Hug Your Teddy Bear

(Tune: Wind The Bobbin' Up)
Hug your teddy bear,
Hug your teddy bear,
Hug, hug, hold him tight.
Smile if you love him,
Smile if you care,
Smile if you love your teddy bear.

Teddy Bear

(Tune: Tommy Thumb)
Teddy bear, teddy bear,
Where are you?
There you are, there you are,
How do you do.
(Repeat with other bears e.g. Polar bear, Grizzly bear, Panda bear, Koala bear etc.)

Teddy Is His Name-O

(Tune: Bingo Was His Name-o)
I have a teddy, I love him and Teddy is his name-o.
T E D D Y, T E D D Y, T E D D Y
And Teddy is his name-o.

Three Bears Dancing On The Beat

(Original tune)
There were three bears dancing on the beat. X3
Dancing down the street.
Daddy bear was dancing on the beat (loud)
Mummy bear was dancing on the beat (medium)
Baby bear was dancing on the beat (quiet)
Dancing down the street.

Change to marching, jumping, hopping, skipping, creeping, etc.

Design, Art and Modelling

Pencils and pens

- *Bear portraits:* Ask children to bring in a special bear. Talk about what their bears look like. What could they use to draw a picture of him? Invite them to draw a portrait of their special bear, using feathery, furry and fluffy strokes and marks.

Paint and print

- *Paw prints:* Use thick paint to create bear paw prints. Use shallow trays and dark paint. Dip thumbs to make the pad of each paw and use each finger to create the tips. Repeat across the paper to make a bear track! Stick tracks around room for children to walk along.
- *Me and my bear:* Take a photograph of each child and their special bear. Create a bear-shaped frame using this template and decorate it with paw prints using pasta shapes, cotton wool buds and sponges as printing tools..

Stepping Stones to Creativity

Collage

- *Collage bears:* Collect together felt, fabrics, sequins and other tactile materials. Use templates (see templates at the back of this book) and cut, shape and stick the materials on to create a furry friend.
- *Bear masks:* Make a bear-shaped face mask using brown/black paper. Experiment with different ways to cut and shape paper by folding, rolling, curling and fringing. Use these to add texture to each bear mask. Can the children tell you what their bear looks like? Is he scary or friendly?

Modelling

- *Knit a Scarf:* Use a commercial French knitting tool to create a long multi-coloured scarf for a bear. Or make your own tool using a cotton reel and four nails tapped into the top and a cocktail stick. Thread the wool from top to bottom and wind the wool around in each pin in an anti-clockwise direction. Wind around each pin in turn and use the stick to lift a loop up and over each pin. Watch the scarf grow.
- *Bear mittens:* Use a variety of paper and card to shape, draw and cut a pair of simple bear mittens. Staple or tape around the edges. Add paw prints on the palm and fur effects on the back to create a pair of paws to wear! Invite children to dress up as bears using the masks and mitts and add some sound effects!

Clay and Dough

- *Model bears:* Use clay/playdough or plasticine to form a bear. Challenge children to combine cylinders, circles and spheres of their chosen material to create a bear. Add furry textures using combs and forks.

Famous Art

E.H. Shepherd - Winnie the Pooh illustrations

Best bear: Ask children to draw a picture of a favourite teddy bear character to illustrate a story using sketching pencils or charcoal. Add colour using watercolour paints.

Dance and Movement

Warm Up

What Bear am I?
Ask the children to think of as many different types of bears as possible including character bears. For example

Polar bears, Grizzly bears, teddy bears, Winnie the Pooh and Paddington Bear. Invite the children to do a short performance of how their chosen bear might move and sound. Can the other children guess what or who they are pretending to be?

Dance

Perform a Song
Invite children to perform the song "The Bear went over the Mountain", "We're going on a Bear Hunt" or "If you go down to the woods today" providing appropriate props and encouragement. Don't demonstrate too much as the idea is to promote children's own creativity.

Bare Necessities
Play the music *"Bare Necessities"* from Disney's Jungle Book and allow the children to create their own dance to match the groovy beat of the music.

Movement Games

Goldilocks and the Three Bears
Similar to "What's the time Mr Wolf?" Three children are chosen to be Daddy, Mummy and Baby Bear. The bears stand at one end of the room or garden with all the other children at the opposite end. The children call out "Who is home today?" and the bears call out Daddy, Mummy or Baby. The children then take a step forward. If the bears call out "Goldilocks" they chase the children until three are caught. These three become the new bears.

Cool Down

Pretend to be a bear getting ready for hibernation. Gather the things you need to make a warm soft bed in your cave. Make sure you have eaten a big supper and settle down, stretching and yawning before you drift into a deep sleep. Encourage the children to describe their actions, what sort of a bear are they, what things are they gathering, what are they eating? What is the weather like?

Clothes

Drama games

- *Pass the hat:* Sing this song as you pass a hat around the circle:

  Who will wear the hat today?   X3
  Who will wear the hat?
  [Tune: In and Out the Dusky Bluebells]

  Whoever is holding the hat at the end of the song has to put it on and assume the character and add a line of dialogue if possible. Try it with two different hats and make up a conversation.

Mime

- *Costume box:* Pack a small suitcase with items of clothing and dressing up clothes. Let children take turns to choose an item to wear and then mime a character or activity for the others to guess.
- *Mirrors:* In pairs ask children to take turns miming putting on different clothes for their partner to mirror. Try hat and scarf, gloves, coat and shoes. See also the Food and Ourselves sections.

Drama skills

- Go on a journey and change clothes according to the different places you visit. Sort out a pair of boots and an umbrella, a sun hat and glasses, hat and scarf, and see how quickly the children can change as they visit the rainforest, the desert and the north pole.
- *Magic hat, slipper or cloak:* Present the clothing to the children and explain that it has magic qualities in that it can make you invisible, clever, able to fly and so on. In small groups improvise drama situations using the magic clothing.

Role-play

The clothes shop

Set up: Clothes on hangers sorted into types and sizes, cash tills, purses, accessories, money, carrier bags, a changing room, a full-length mirror. Change the setting to a shoe shop and add lots of different types of shoes in boxes and shoe-measuring equipment.

Roles: Shop assistant, customers.

Stories: A rude customer or shop assistant; a hard to please customer; a customer who doesn't fit any of the clothes; returning a faulty item; a fashion show. Act out the traditional story of *The Elves and The Shoemaker.*

Stories

The Elves and the Shoemaker Traditional
Make moving puppets for the elves from cardboard shapes and split pins.
Act out the story using children and puppets.

Cinderella Traditional
Draw designs for Cinderella's rags and ballgown.

Mrs Lather's Laundry by Allan Ahlberg
Sing the washing song below.

Little Robin Red Vest by Jan Fearnley
Act out the story as Robin gives away his seven vests to all his friends to help them keep warm.

Songs and rhymes

- Dingle-Dangle Scarecrow
- My Hat It Has Three Corners
- Down In The Jungle
- Cobbler Cobbler

Washing Song

(Tune: Here We Go Round The Mulberry Bush)
This is the way we wash the clothes,
Wash the clothes, wash the clothes.
This is the way we wash the clothes,
In the washing machine.

Watch them whirling round and round,
Round and round, round and round,
Watch them whirling round and round,
In the washing machine.

I can...

(Tune: Polly Put The Kettle On)
I can put my coat on X3
And do the buttons too.

I can tie my shoes up X3
Can I help you?

What Are You Wearing Today?

(Tune: Hickory Dickory Dock)
What are you wearing today?
What are you wearing today?
My coat and hat, coat and hat,
That's what I'm wearing today.
Try other pairs of clothes

Clothes Rhyme

Coats and shirts,
Trousers and skirts,
All my clothes are shrinking!
Shoes and tops,
Jumpers and socks,
But instead I'm thinking,
There's no way of knowing.
Perhaps it's me that's growing?

Design, Art and Modelling

Pencils and pens

- *D.I.Y. shirts:* Help children to draw pictures, designs, patterns and words on plain coloured cotton t-shirts. This can be linked to a special day or fundraising event. Let them practise on paper first! Also works on canvas shoes or fabric bags.
- *Fashion designers:* Look at photographs of different clothes. Make sketches of clothes and have fun designing fantastic new outfits.

Paint and print

- *Shoelace painting:* Use string, shoe laces, cord, or chains to paint. Help children to hold string with a clothes peg and dip it into trays of paint. Lift out onto paper and move around. Fold over the paper or place a second piece on top, press down and pull out the string.
- *Welly printing:* Find some Wellington boots with interesting patterns on the soles. Invite children to step into a shallow tray of paint and then walk along a roll of lining paper to make welly prints.

Collage

- *Collage gear:* Draw round the body of a child on large piece of paper. Design, cut, stick and create clothes using different fabrics. Accessorise with buttons, zips, Velcro, ribbons and bows to practice fastening.

Modelling

- *In print:* Make coats or tabards out of newspaper. Use broad sheets folded in half with a hole cut out for the head. Try folding sheets of newspaper into hats. Cover boots with a layer of torn pieces of newspaper and glue (papier mâché).
- *Designer hats:* Use lots of different materials to create designer hats. Decorate plain straw or felt hats with feathers, silk flowers, netting, beads and buttons. Try tall conical hats, or simple origami folded hats. Organise a fashion parade.

Clay and dough

- *Milliner's art:* Make hats out of playdough for finger people or small plastic dolls. Decorate with sequins and beads. At the other end, try moulding shoes around doll's feet.

- *Fancy pendants:* Cut small shapes from clay or salt and flour dough. Punch a tiny hole in the top using a straw. Decorate with a child's initial, name or simple picture. Bake or dry before painting. Thread onto a leather thong and wear with pride!

Famous Art

Pierre Auguste Renoir - Luxembourg Garden

Look at and discuss the children's clothes in the painting. How is the fabric shown? What would the clothes feel like? Ask children to draw or paint a favourite piece of clothing.

Dance and Movement

Warm Up

Coloured Clothes
(Sung to the tune of Frère Jacques)

Children wearing blue x 2
Please stand up X 2
Do your own groovy thing X 2
Then sit down X 2

Sing any colour the children choose. Children wearing that colour stand up and dance. Repeat with different colours to ensure all children who want a turn get an opportunity to perform.

Dance

"Auntie Monica"
Perform the song. If possible give the children dressing up clothes to encourage participation and movement.

Dressing up
Play a wide variety of music such as Waltz, Tango, Salsa, Pop, Latin, Irish, Pan Pipes and Classical, the wider the variety the better. Have a box of scarves, hats, shoes, bags and floating materials for the children to play and dance with. The aim is to encourage the children's own creativity to the music.

Movement Games

Egyptian Mummies
The aim of the game is to wrap a friend as an Egyptian mummy using any material you like – strips of crepe paper or newspaper, white fabric, bandages or even toilet paper. Play music whilst children complete the task before the music stops.

Cool Down

Make believe you have a basket of giant clothes that need to be sorted and folded. Give the children colossal imaginary jumpers and trousers to fold and make neat. They may need to work in small teams as if folding bed sheets.

Colours

Drama games

- Develop speaking and listening skills by making up colourful tongue-twisters such as 'big beautiful blue balloon burst with a bang' and 'red pepper, yellow pepper, green pepper, blue, pick a coloured capsicum and cook it for me too'.
- *Changing places:* Stand in a circle and call out "change places if you're wearing red". Choose different colours and see how quickly the children can move.
- *Introductions:* Go round the circle taking turns to introduce yourself and tell the group what your favourite colour is. For example 'my name is Joel and my favourite colour is purple.'

Mime

- *Moody colours:* Talk about colours and moods. Choose facial expressions for each colour or mood: red for angry, blue for sad, green for jealous, yellow for scared, orange for happy, and black for moody. Show a coloured card and ask the children to respond. Extend the activity by thinking up actions for each colour as well, such as jumping for orange and stamping for red.

Drama skills

- Act out the story of *Little Red Riding Hood*. Would the story change if the colour of the cloak was different?

- *Colourful dramas:* Extend some of the ideas from Moody colours into paired dramas. Each child takes on a colour to reflect their mood and make up a story. What might happen when the blue boy meets the yellow boy? Could the red girl be cheered up by the orange girl?

Role-play

Colour swap shop

Set up: Toys and different items sorted into colours, coloured cards, shelving, signs in different colours.

Roles: Shopkeeper, customers, Rainbow Fairy.

Stories: In the swap shop children can swap coloured cards for an item of the same colour. The naughty Rainbow Fairy comes along and mixes all the colours up! Colours

Stories

Little Red Riding Hood Traditional
Act out the story wearing the red cape.
Have fun pretending to be the wolf.

The Mixed-Up Chameleon by Eric Carle
Cut or tear out paper from a magazine and ask children to design their own chameleons.

Little Robin Red Vest by Jan Fearnley
Create a dance for all the animals wearing Robin's different coloured vests

The Rainbow Fish by Marcus Pfister
Paint pictures of rainbow fishes with one shiny scale each.

Songs and rhymes

- I Can Sing A Rainbow
- Lavender's Blue
- Little Boy Blue
- In And Out The Dusky Bluebells

What's Your Favourite Colour?

(Tune: One Man Went To Mow)
Play this game with me,
What's your favourite colour?
Play this game, what's the same
As your favourite colour?
Red: tomatoes, apples, fire engines, ladybirds, peppers, poppies.

Dilly Dilly

(Tune: Lavender's Blue)
Daffodils are yellow
Dilly dilly
Roses are red.
Cornflowers are blue
Dilly dilly
In my flower bed.

Apples are green
Dilly dilly
Strawberries are red
Bananas are yellow
Dilly dilly
Now you are fed.
Emeralds are green
Dilly dilly
Sapphires are blue.
Rubies are red
Dilly dilly,
Rich stones for you.

Spotting Colours

Hop for yellow
Stretch for blue
Spotting colours, one and two.
Shout for orange
Sit for brown
Look for colours all around.
Wink for pink
Whisper for white
Lots of colours, what a sight!
Jump for red
Crouch for green
How many colours have you seen?

Design, Art and Modelling

Pencils and pens

● *Rainbows:* Use an elastic band to join a bundle of pencils or pens together. Help children to draw a rainbow shape across the page using all the pencils at once.

Paint and print

● *Mixing colours:* Put three blobs of primary colours onto a piece of paper and use plastic or card combs to twist,

sweep and scrape the colours together. Watch as the colours mix and new colours emerge.

- *Paint umbrellas:* Cut out large circle shapes and divide into segments like an umbrella. Remind children to take time and care to paint a different colour into each segment. What happens if one colour of paint is not allowed to dry before another is added next to it?

Collage

- *Leaky mosaic:* Cut or tear crepe or tissue paper into small pieces. Place onto a large sheet of white paper and then dab a mixture of water and vinegar onto each piece. When dry, remove the crepe paper and admire the mosaic pattern that is left where the dye leaked out.
- *Colour collage:* Choose a favourite colour and find as many different textured materials of that colour to use in a colour collage.

Modelling

- *Stripey stick:* Go for a walk with the children and look for funny shaped sticks. Wrap short lengths of coloured wool around, regularly changing colours to create a stripey sculpture rather like a snake. Add dangly beads or buttons to create a 3D effect. Alternatively, fasten two sticks into a cross shape and then weave wool under and over the sticks starting from the centre. Change colours and make a woollen eye.

Clay and dough

- *Rainbow dough:* Provide lots of different coloured dough or plasticine. Ask children to make lots of cylinders of dough and shape into a rainbow. Have fun mixing the colours and making new ones. Watch how the colours start by marbling and then continue until the colours blend together into new ones.

Famous Art

Paul Klee – Flora on Sand

Watery colour: Observe and discuss the colours in the painting. Which are the darkest or lightest? Mix paint in different consistencies and paint in blocks of colour. Which colours do the children think go well together? Can they tell you which is the darkest/lightest colour in their picture?

Dance and Movement

Warm Up

Coloured Clothes Song
– see colours topic

Dance

♪ I can dance a rainbow
Gather the children in a circle. In the middle place coloured scarves appropriate to the song "I can sing a rainbow". Invite some children to dance with the scarves whilst the other children sing the song changing the word "sing" to "dance". Give all children an opportunity to perform.

♪ The colours of the wind
You will need a copy of the popular piece of music from the Walt Disney film, Pocahontas. Simply provide children with a clear open space to dance and move about any way they choose.

♪ Yellow Submarine
As above with the Beatles track "The Yellow Submarine"

Movement Games

Colour Swap
Children form a circle standing or sitting. You call out a colour. Those children wearing the colour swap places with another child as quickly as possible. Encourage children to swap places in different ways e.g. red kangaroos. All children wearing red pretend to be jumping kangaroos as they move to swap places.

Cool Down

Stretch up to the blue sky. Bend down to the green grass. Stretch out wide like the yellow sun. Curl up small like the silver moon. Invite children's suggestions to match movement to objects around them.

Dinosaurs

Drama and Role Play

Drama games

- *Action/Freeze:* Ask children to find a space in the room and when you shout 'action' to move freely around taking care not to bump into anybody. When you shout 'freeze' they must all stand still like a statue. Then ask them to work in pairs and create contrasting dinosaur statues – tall and short, big and small, carnivores and herbivores, spiky and smooth, fast and slow.

Mime

- *Moving dinosaurs:* Talk about different sorts of dinosaurs such as carnivores, herbivores, flying dinosaurs and so on. Ask children to think of different ways to move for each dinosaur.

Drama skills

- *The dinosaur egg:* Improvise a drama about a group of children who discover a large plastic egg while on a picnic. Talk about the characters and plan and prepare the picnic food. Then travel to the picnic in the forest once you find the egg let the children decide what to do with it. Should they leave it alone, take it home, or break it? Narrate the ending – make sure the egg is returned to where they found it so that when the mother dinosaur comes back to find it out hatches a baby dinosaur!
- *We're all going on a dinosaur hunt:* Adapt the well-known rhyme about the bear hunt to include dinosaurs!

Role-play

The dinosaur museum

Set up: Create displays of dinosaur bones or pictures. Tickets, cloakroom, leaflets, a recorded museum guide, museum shop with toys and postcards. Make model dinosaurs as exhibits from wire, modroc, papier mache and paint.

Roles: Curator, tour guides, visitors, teacher, school party, dinosaurs.

Stories: Night at the museum – the dinosaur exhibits come to life! A school trip to the museum in which a child gets lost or breaks an exhibit. Set up a new display with an exciting new dinosaur that has just been discovered.

Stories, Songs and Rhymes

Stories

Tyrannosaurus Drip by Julia Donaldson
Make model dinosaurs out of salt and flour dough or clay. Paint the models in bright colours.

Bumpus Jumpus Dinosaurumpus by Tony Mitton
Have fun reciting the rhyming text and add sound effects.

The Dance of the Dinosaurs by Colin Hawkins
Create a dinosaur dance with the children.

Harry and the Bucketful of Dinosaurs by Ian Whybrow
Act out the story using a plastic bucket and some small toy dinosaurs.

Songs and rhymes

I Saw A Dinosaur
I thought I saw a dinosaur,
I thought I heard its mighty roar,
I thought I felt its sharp claw,
But do you know what is weird?
I really saw a dinosaur,
I really heard its mighty roar,
I really felt its sharp claw,
And then it disappeared!

Five Fierce Dinosaurs
(Tune: Ten Green Bottles)
Five fierce dinosaurs standing in a row X2
And if one fierce dinosaur should flick his tail and go
There'd be four fierce dinosaurs standing in a row...

Dina The Dinosaur
(Tune: Hey Diddle Diddle)
Dina the dinosaur
Sat on the river floor
And dined on dinner at ten

She ate some fish
From a silvery dish
And then ran back home again.

Dina the dinosaur
Opened her giant jaw
Then began to roar
She lay down to rest
In a cosy nest
And soon began to snore.

Design, Art and Modelling

Pencils and pens

- *Dino drawings:* Provide a range of simple dinosaur outlines or stencils and use a range of drawing materials: pens, pencils and wax crayons, etc. Ask children to explore how many dinosaur patterns they can make? Try speckled, striped, and scaly.

Paint and print

- *Footprints:* Help children to cut medium-sized potatoes into half. Use one half to print dino feet. Use the edge of the remaining half to form toes/claws. Cut into further smaller circles or triangles. Print different sized dino footprints on large sheets of paper.
- *Dinosaur walkabout:* Provide a collection of plastic dinosaurs. Dip their feet into paint-filled trays and walk them across a piece of paper. Where will the tracks go? Add background trees, bushes, paths, undergrowth and water for the dinosaurs to trail past.

Collage

- *Textured dinosaurs:* Provide simple dinosaur shapes cut out of thin card/cereal packets. Cover using a range of materials: corrugated card, bubble wrap, egg boxes, chocolate box trays, etc. Arrange the materials and stick down using tape and pva glue.

Modelling

- *Junk dinosaurs:* Encourage children to choose and join junk to make dinosaur models. Use egg boxes, tubes, and cartons. Fix together and paint.
- *Dinosaur eggs:* Help children to blow up balloons and cover in papier mâché and modroc to create giant egg shapes. Leave to dry and then paint with speckly and

swirly shapes. Place in a shredded paper nest and wait for them to hatch!

Clay and dough

- *Clay models:* Use small plastic dinosaurs to discuss body shapes: legs, wings, horns, spines and heads. Invite children to make bodies and body parts to create a dinosaur. Use bent pipe cleaners to add spikes and horns.

Famous Art

BBC Walking with dinosaurs

Dinosaur landscape: On a large sheet of card or tray scrunch up paper to create hills and valleys. Cover in modroc and paint with green and brown paint textured with sand. Use as a play area for plastic or clay dinosaurs!

Goto www.abc.net.au/dinosaurs - an excellent website set up to accompany the BBC series with videos, stills and games.

Dance and Movement

Warm Up

 Similar to the Sleeping Bunnies activity. Children lie down on the floor and pretend to be sleeping dinosaurs.

See the little dinosaurs sleeping till its noon
See if we can wake them with this little tune
Hark how still, are they ill?
Wake up soon
Wake up little dinos
STOMP little dinos STOMP STOMP STOMP x 3
STOMP little dinos STOMP STOMP and stop.

Dance

Dino Dance
Play some of the children's favourite music and do a silly dinosaur dance. Bop like a Brachiosaurs, tango as a T-Rex, party as a Parasaurolophus, salsa as a Stegosaurus or tap dance as a Triceratops!

You may want to dance along to dinosaur themed music such as;
Harry and his bucket of dinosaurs
Barney the Dinosaur
Dinosaur Music by Schott Steaedt

Movement Games

Dino Dash
Gather the children together outdoors and ask them to collect materials to create a large square on the ground – leaves, twigs, pine cones, pebbles etc. One child is T-Rex. The rest are plant eating dinosaurs frightened of T-Rex. T-Rex aims to tag the plant eaters. Once tagged, they lie down. The last one to be tagged becomes T-Rex. Children stay within the marked square.

Dino footprints
Have the children create large dinosaur footprints using various creative materials such as construction paper, paints, pens, glitter, newspaper and so on. Tape the footprints around the room on the floor. Play music and encourage children to dance from one footprint to another. Stop the music. Any child not on a footprint imagines being stuck in the swamp until the next go.

Cool Down

Imagine you are a baby dinosaur emerging from your egg. You are in a quiet peaceful nest tapping gently on the shell. Come out of the shell slowly and tentatively stretching each of your limbs. Maybe you are weak on your new legs and struggle to walk before going to explore your environment.

Families

Drama games

- *Family voices:* Encourage children to use different voices to answer the question 'can you use a daddy voice?' Change the question to mummy, baby, granddad, angry aunty, unhappy uncle, silly sister, bossy brother etc.
- *One-line family characters:* Sit in a circle and ask children to think of something mum or dad might say. Go round and invite them to deliver a 'one-line character' for others to guess. Extend by adding a mood such as angry, sad, happy or impatient.

Mime

- *Family freeze frames:* Explain that you are going to arrange the children into family groups and then take pretend pictures of them. Ask each group to talk and interact with each other and then shout 'freeze' as a signal to be still. Try inventing different family situations such as a celebratory meal, an outing, an argument etc.

Drama skills

- *Two Fat Gentlemen:* Learn the finger rhyme, as shown below, and then use as a framework for different family characters such as: two old granddads, two thin mummies, two tall daddies, two teen sisters, and two naughty babies. Number the characters 1 – 5 and then mix and match the numbers to create new dramatic situations where number 1, the old granddad, meets number 4, the teen sister, and so on.

The Two Fat Gentlemen Finger Rhyme

Two fat gentlemen
Met in a lane

Bowed most politely
And bowed once again

And said 'How do you do?'

And 'How do you do?' again.

Role-play

The home corner

Set up: Usual home corner furniture, baby dolls, camera, presents, baby equipment: food, clothes, wipes, toys, bottles, high chair, buggy, cot, changing-mat, bath, towels.

Roles: Mum, dad, children, baby, grandparents, aunts, uncles, neighbours and friends.

Stories: New baby in the family. Act out the baby coming home: how does everyone in the family feel? The baby cries a lot and nobody can sleep! Everyone has to be quiet so baby can sleep and every little noise wakes him up! Tidy up the house ready for visitors. Organise a celebration or party in the house.

Stories

 Dr. Xargle's Book of Earthlets by Jeanne Willis
Design and paint an alien family.

 Big Book of Families by Catherine Anholt
Paint a portrait of your own family from a photograph.

 Tell Me What It's Like To Be Big by Joyce Dunbar
Act out Willa's attempts to 'do things for herself'.

 Grandad Pot by Siobhan Dodds
Act out the story as Grandad cooks lots of food for Polly and her friends.

Songs and rhymes

- Here Are Grandma's Glasses
- There Were Ten In The Bed
- Tommy Thumb
- Jack Sprat
- There Was An Old Woman Who Lived In A Shoe
- Rock-A-Bye Baby

The Family's In The Ring
(Tune: Farmers In His Den)
The family's in the ring

The family's in the ring
E I E I
The family's in the ring.

The father wants a wife…
The wife wants a child…
The child wants a sister/brother…

In My Family
(Tune: Oh My Darling)
In my family, in my family,
There are three of us you see.
Mum and dad, mum and dad,
And me makes three.
Plus my sister, plus my sister,
Altogether that makes four.
And my nana, and my nana,
No there are not any more.
In my family, in my family,
There are five of us you know.
Wait a minute, wait a minute,
Should I count the baby too?

Design, Art and Modelling

Pencils and pens

- *Family strings:* Help children to fold paper into a concertina shape and then cut out strings of people making sure not to cut through the folds. Ask children to decorate the people with faces, hair and colourful clothes to represent all the people in their family.
- *Happy families:* Use different coloured felt pens to draw faces on children's finger tips and let them nod, bow and dance.

Paint and print

- *Family portraits:* Ask children to bring in photographs of their family. Paint big pictures of all the people in the family.
- *Posh frames:* Cut frame shapes out of card. Fill squeezy bottles with PVA glue and make sure that it will come out easily. If necessary cut a larger hole in the nozzle. Squirt patterns in glue all over the frame. Allow to dry and then paint on top with gold acrylic paint for a special frame for the family portraits.

Collage

- *Stick and straw family:* Provide a selection of matchsticks, cocktail sticks, straws and lollipop sticks cut to a variety

of lengths to create a stick and straw family. Add circle heads and faces and stick them down onto a card. Let children take the cards home for their families.

Modelling

- *Dolly-peg families:* Use old-fashioned clothes pegs, pipe cleaners, fabric and pens to create a family. Ask children to give them all names?

Clay and dough

- *Animal families:* Make a series of different-sized balls of dough and form them into a family of snakes, mice or hedgehogs. Start with the biggest or 'daddy', followed by 'mummy', then getting smaller and smaller until left with the tiny baby!

Famous Art

Henry Moore – Family Group
All shapes and sizes!: Use this sculpture as a starting point for plasticine work. Ask children to make a family like this one. Who are the figures in their sculpture? How does this sculpture make them feel? Photograph the families and display alongside the artist's own.

Pablo Picasso – Mother & Child

Crayon cuddles: Look at the drawing and talk about who is in it? What is happening? How does it make them feel? Discuss who gives us cuddles and invite them to draw or paint themselves having a cuddle with a special person!

Dance and Movement

Warm Up

 Imagine you are a big strong Daddy – how might he move about? Imagine you are a beautiful, happy Mummy – how might she move about? Imagine you are a tiny baby or an old Granddad – how might they move about? Children could mime their own relations.

Dance

 Perform the song The Wheels On The Bus with children finding actions for all the passengers:

Mummies	Daddies	Grandparents
Babies	Children	Teenagers

Perform the Farmers In The Dell encouraging children to use members of their own families instead of the traditional verses e.g. the farmer has a cousin or the wife has a sister.

Five big daddies I once knew
Tall ones, fat ones, skinny ones too
But the one in the middle that belongs to me
I love him and he loves me
Down to the football we must go
With a wibble wobble wibble wobble to and fro
But the one in the middle that belongs to me
I love him and he loves me

Five happy mummies I once knew
Tall ones, fat ones, skinny ones too
But the one in the middle that belongs to me
I love her and she loves me
Down to the shops we must go with a wibble
wobble wibble wobble to and fro
But the one in the middle that belongs to me
I love her and she loves me
Sing and perform to the tune of "Six little ducks".

Encourage children to create their own movements for this song.

Movement Games

Parachute Swap

 Stand holding the edge of a parachute. Go around the parachute and give each child a title of daddy, mummy, brother or sister. Call out one of the titles e.g. daddy. All children named daddy must run under the parachute and out the other side. Find different ways of moving under the parachute. Invite children's suggestions.

Cool Down

Perform Rock A Bye Baby or Hush Little Baby, as a group. If possible give the children dolls to use as babies.

Stepping Stones to Creativity

Farms

Drama and Role Play

Drama games

- Sit in a circle and pass round farm animal sounds trying not to repeat each other. Add suitable actions.
- *Action/freeze:* Ask children to find a space to stand in. Make sure they cannot touch anybody near them and that they have plenty of space to move around. When you shout out 'action' invite them to move around freely until you shout 'freeze'. Then they must freeze and pretend to be a farm animal statue or scarecrow of their choice.

Mime

- *Down on the farm:* Ask children to take turns miming different farm animals for the group to guess. Add a farmer and mime how we use the different animals on the farm such as milking a cow or riding a horse.
- Pass a pretend piece of food around the circle. Start with an orange that needs to be peeled and eaten segment by segment. Pass it to the next child and let them mime a different piece of food such as a crunchy carrot, banana, or strawberry. Can the others guess what is being eaten each time?

Drama skills

- *Scary scarecrows:* Talk about scarecrows. Ask the children to pose as a scarecrow; very still but with a scary face! Improvise a dramatic story about scarecrows who come to life. Are they friendly or not? Go into role as a chief scarecrow and direct the story if necessary. The scarecrows could work together to save the farm from being built on, or gang together to scare away the farmer.

Role-play

The farm and farm shop

Set up: Home corner with lots of cooking utensils, a model fire made from tissue paper, cellophane, and newspaper. An outside area with sit-and-ride toys including a tractor, a field of crops made from corrugated cardboard. A farm shop with shelves, tables, real or pretend fruit and vegetables, bread, homemade biscuits, plant pots, tools etc.

Make fruit using screwed up newspaper, modroc and paint. Make real biscuits to sell at the farm shop.

Roles: Farmer, farmer's wife, children, workers, animals, shop assistants, customers, school children.

Stories: School trip to visit the farm or shop; a lost animal; the discovery of new mystery fruit or vegetable; harvesting crops on the farm for theharvest festival; making bread. Act out the traditional stories *The Little Red Hen* or *The Enormous Turnip*.

Stories, Songs and Rhymes

Stories

The Enormous Turnip Traditional
Act out the story as the farmer, his family and lots of animals try to lift the turnip. Add sound effects.

Farmer Duck by Martin Waddell
Act out the story with all the animals doing the work.

The Pig in the Pond by Martin Waddell
Collect together paintings or drawings of all the different farm animals and mount them into a large group collage with scrunched up cling film and plastic for the water.

The Little Red Hen Traditional
Make some bread and sing the song on the following page.

Songs and rhymes

- I Went To Visit A Farm One Day
- Old Macdonald Had A Farm
- Baa Baa Black Sheep
- The Farmer's In His Dell
- One Man Went To Mow
- Oat And Beans And Barley Grow

Ten Little Piglets On The Farm
(Tune: Ten Little Indians)
There was one, there were two
There were three little piglets
There were four, there were five
There were six little piglets,
There were seven, there were eight,
There were nine little piglets
Ten little piglets on the farm.

Repeat with different animals

Down On The Farm.
(Tune: The Wheels On The Bus)
The cows in the barn say moo, moo, moo
Moo, moo, moo, moo, moo, moo
The cows in the barn say moo, moo, moo
Down on the farm.

Try with different farm animals

Little Hen Wants To Make Some Bread
(Tune: Here We Go Round The Mulberry Bush)
Little hen wants to make some bread,
Make some bread, make some bread.
Little hen wants to make some bread.
Poor little red hen.

This is the way she plants the seed...
This is the way she grinds the corn…
This is the way she bakes the bread…
Little red hen won't share the bread…

Design, Art and Modelling

Pencils and pens

- *Design a scarecrow:* Ask children to draw a picture of a crazy scarecrow that is guaranteed to scare everyone and everything away!
- *Farmer's Fields:* Fold a square of paper into quarters and use a range of drawing media to create a field of furrows in each section. See how many different types of furrows children can create. Try straight, zigzag, wavy and wriggly!

Paint and print

- *Aerial squares:* Use aerial photographs of the countryside to observe the patterns and shapes made by fields and hedges. What are the colours of the countryside? Use a large sheet of paper (or several smaller ones stuck together!) to sponge and print fields and hedges.
- *Animal prints:* Use plastic animal shaped cutters dipped in trays of paint to print farm animals on the paper fields.

Collage

- *Patchwork fields:* Look at aerial pictures of fields. Take a piece of cardboard and divide into 6 sections. Invite children to choose a different textured and coloured material to cover each field. Use as a play mat for plastic farm animals.

Stepping Stones to Creativity

Modelling

- *Woolly sheep:* Help children to cut out a sheep shape using the template (see templates at the back of this book). Wrap black or white wool round and round the body of the sheep until the body is nice and fat. Fasten off with tape. Count and stick the sheep into a giant field and use as a display.
- *Money-box pig:* Help children to blow up a small balloon and cover with a layer of papier mâché. Attach egg cartons for the snout and legs and cover in two more layers of paper. Leave to dry. Cut a slit in the top for the coins and a hole in the base. Paint and add a curly pipe cleaner tail.

Clay and dough

- *Curly sheep:* Form model sheep bodies from dough. Push balls of dough through a garlic press to create strings of wool on top. Ask children to try and design other farm animals.
- *2D animal farm:* Use salt flour dough to make model animals. Use cutters to make 2D shapes. Bake and then paint.

Famous Art

Vincent Van Gogh - Landscape with House and Ploughman

Chalk Farm: Talk about the shapes and textures in the painting. Chalk a birds-eye view farm onto a flat, concrete surface. Work in groups to add different textures, hay and straw. Add fences and animals, maybe even a ploughman!

Dance and Movement

Warm Up

 Let's pretend the cockerel has lost his voice and you must wake up the animals on the farm. Using handheld instruments begin by trying to gently wake the animals. Sitting, encourage children to shake and bang quietly. The animals are still not awake so get up and walk around the farm making instruments sound louder and louder. Can the children create a rhythm or invent a song as they go?

Dance

The Farmer's in his Dell and The Dingle Dangle Scarecrow

Children love to perform the Farmer's in his Dell and The Dingle Dangle Scarecrow. Simply sing them for yourselves or dance along to a children's cd.

Old MacDonald had a farm

Perform this song moving around a room or outdoor area. A child is chosen to be the farmer. The other children follow the farmer around the room whilst singing and acting out the actions of all the animals.

Movement Games

Who am I?

See the activity in the Animals topic and use farm animals instead.

The scarecrow game

A child is chosen to be the scarecrow. They stand in the middle of the room or outside area. The other children are crows and stand around the edge of the area. The scarecrow stands with arms outstretched and pretends to be asleep. The crows must move quietly towards the sleeping scarecrow. If the scarecrow awakens the crows must stand perfectly still. If they move they return to the edge of the area. The aim is to be the first to reach the scarecrow. The scarecrow can shout "Get off my land" at any time and the crows must fly away screaming!

Traditional sack race

Children climb into sacks and jump from a starting line to a finishing line. As they jump, mime and make the sound of a chosen farm animal.

Cool Down

 If possible set up an area with hay or straw for the children to lie down and rest in while you perform the following songs: Little Boy Blue, Litter Bo Peep and This Little Piggy Went to Market. Cushions make a good alternative.

Flight

Drama and Role Play

Drama games

- Ask children to stand in a space in the room. Explain that they are to move around slowly and carefully, not bumping into anybody else when they hear the slow drum beat. As the tempo changes and the drum beat speeds up ask them to pretend to fly around on tiptoes still taking care not to touch anyone else.
- *Balloons:* Blow up a balloon as children watch and then release the air carefully. Ask the children to pretend to inflate as you blow into the balloon and then slowly deflate. Repeat, and this time let the balloon go so that it whizzes around! Can they do the same and add sound effects?

Mime

- *Magic carpet:* Sit in a circle and ask the children to close their eyes as you narrate a journey on a magic carpet. Start with a flight to the children's own bedrooms to select a favourite toy or book. Describe where the carpet is flying over and end the journey with a recognised phrase such as 'the carpet landed with a bump and a tumble!' Go on flights to other places and countries. This is a really good way of helping children to concentrate and enter their dramatic imagination.

Drama skills

- *In a hot air balloon:* Improvise a drama from the air. A group of characters go on an early morning flight in a hot air balloon and witness something bad happening on the ground below. Can they do anything to stop it?

Role-play

The airport

Set up: An airplane – put pairs of seats in a row with an aisle down the middle. Open a check-in desk with tickets, passports, uniforms, a luggage conveyer belt, an x-ray machine for hand baggage. Open a shop or café in the airport waiting area.

Roles: Pilot, stewards, passengers, airport workers, porters.

Stories: Late to catch a plane, delays to flight and have to sleep in the airport, grumpy passengers, find something strange in a passenger's luggage.

Stories, Songs and Rhymes

Stories

Pigs Might Fly by Jonathan Emmett
Design and build model planes from recycled materials for the three little pigs.

Kite Flying by Grace Lin
Make up a kite dance, making stretching and curling body shapes to floaty music.

The Firebird Traditional
Design a collage picture of a firebird using feathers, paint, sequins, and sparkly materials.

Amazing Airplanes by Tony Mitton
Make a wall display of a giant plane with a window showing each child's face.

The Owl Babies by Martin Waddell
Act out the story and learn the 'Three Little Owls' Rhyme.

Songs and rhymes

- Two Little Dicky Birds
- Five Little Ducks Went Swimming One Day

Oh When The Plane

(Tune: Oh When The Saints)
Oh when the plane
Goes flying by
Oh when the plane
Goes flying by
I want to be in that airplane
As it flies high in the sky.

My Airplane

(Tune: My Bonnie)
The aeroplane flies over the ocean
The aeroplane flies over the sea
The aeroplane flies back to the airport
And brings back my home to me.

Five Fat Blackbirds

(Tune: Ten Green Bottles)
Five fat blackbirds sitting in a tree
Five fat blackbirds sitting in a tree
And if one fat blackbird should fly away free
There'd be four fat blackbirds sitting in a tree.

Three Little Owls

Three little owls in a nest in a tree
Are very, very hungry, as hungry as can be.
Mother owl goes hunting, at night goes she.
Three little owls in a nest in a tree.

Three little owls in a nest in a tree
Missing their mother, as lonely as can be.
Mother owl returns with food for all three.
Three little owls in a nest in a tree.

Design, Art and Modelling

Pencils and pens

- *Airport runways:* Provide black sugar paper cut into thin strips and coloured chalks/pastels. Look at images of airports and runways at night. Make patterns of different coloured lights on the paper runway.

Paint and print

- *Kites:* Help children to cut out a variety of traditional (diamond) and modern kite shapes. How are they decorated? Divide the kite into sections and paint in bright colours. Add a tail or eyes! Decorate the tail with small bows cut from paper.
- *Feathers:* Use a collection of sturdy feathers and thick paint. Dip the feathers into the paint and experiment with the different ways to use them: the tip, the end, the sides, etc.

Collage

- *Hot air balloons:* Make a brightly patterned balloon using a template (see templates at the back of this book) or cover a partially inflated balloon with papier mâché. Cover in paper and plastic. Attach a basket using strings or elastic. Use straw, twigs and twisted paper to create a collage basket. Hang from the ceiling.

Modelling

- *Dream catchers:* Provide hoops made from garden wire or old wire coat hangers. Wind coloured strings and wool around the hoop, securing it each time on the edge by wrapping around a few times. Working in all directions make a web. Hang a few more pieces of string onto the bottom and use feathers and beads to finish.
- *Junk model aeroplanes:* Ask children to make a plane or helicopter using thin strips of balsa wood, lolly sticks, straws, cardboard, nails and glue. Make helicopter blades using 2 lollysticks in a cross position and attach to the top of a box using a split pin. Add a cardboard tube for the tail.

Clay and dough

- *Two little dicky birds:* Use clay or dough to make two model birds and invite children to act out this well-known rhyme. Alternatively, build a wall from dough bricks and use fingers in the traditional way to say the rhyme!

Famous Art

Paul Klee – Red Balloon

Pastel shapes: Experiment with using pastels lengthways to make squares, circles and rectangles. Make balloon shapes and use the tip of the pastel to draw a thin string.

of how wind direction works as children will see their props moving very differently to if the dance were performed indoors.

Movement games

Let's go fly a kite
Carrier bags tied on long lengths of string or ribbon make quick and easy kites for outdoor fun.

Catching Bubbles
Children adore playing with bubbles. A bubble machine will provide a plentiful supply of bubbles for children to move about, jumping and running to catch and pop the bubbles. This activity is great played outdoors and gives a whole different dimension to how the bubbles move about.

Cool Down

Imagine you are blowing up a giant balloon. Take deep breaths in before slowly blowing up your imaginary balloon. Move your arms as if they are the balloon getting bigger and bigger before clapping your hands together to pop it. Invite children to tell you what colour balloon they are going to blow up or what imaginary pattern the balloon has on it.

Dance and Movement

Warm Up

Imagine you are birds flying high in the sky. Encourage elegant flowing movements swooping and gliding through the air gracefully and peacefully. Ask the children what type of bird they are pretending to be. Alternatively imagine you are a kite, a plane or a hot air balloon.

Dance

Flying machines
Invite children to become a flying machine and to move around the room in their own unique way. Music from Chitty Chitty Bang Bang the musical makes good background music for this activity, encouraging children to match movements to music.

Floating
Using music that gives an ambience of floating, provide children with streamers, bubbles or balloons to dance with. Dance performed outdoors will give children an understanding

Food

Drama games

- *I went to the market:* This is a good game for concentration and listening skills. Go round the circle asking each person to add an item of food they bought at the market to the list. See the topic on Shopping for related games.
- *Fruit salad:* Stand in a circle and give each child the name of one of three or four different fruits such as apples, grapes, oranges, bananas. When you call out each type of fruit they must change places. On the signal 'fruit salad' everybody must move!
- *Beans:* Use the names of different beans to initiate actions: runner beans – run on the spot; broad beans – stand with hands and feet spread side; string beans – stand with body stretched as tall as possible; jelly beans – wobble like jelly; baked beans – curl up small on the floor, and so on.

Mime

- *Mirrors:* Work in pairs and mime eating food in a mirror. Try messy food such as pasta, packets of crisps or chewy toffee. Partners must try to mirror all the facial expressions and hand movements. See the topics of Clothes and Ourselves.
- *Chewing gum:* Pretend to chew gum with your mouth closed, stretching all the facial muscles and pulling lots of silly faces. Ask children to join in and then remove gum and pretend that it's stuck to your finger and won't

shake off. Have fun as the gum gets stuck to your toes, nose, ear, legs and use as a general physical warm up!

Drama skills

- *The market stall:* Improvise a drama about a busy market stall selling lots of different food. Help children to make up market calls for their wares. Encourage them to project their voices. Introduce situations involving difficult customers, a thief and bad weather.

Role-play

Café or restaurant

Set up: Tables, chairs, tablecloths, menus, vases of flowers, real and pretend food, crockery, and a blackboard for specials! Organise a kitchen area with a cooker, sink, place to prepare food etc. Introduce a particular cuisine such as Chinese, Indian, Italian or healthy food. Change into a fast-food restaurant.

Roles: Waiter, waitress, chef, customers.

Stories: The kitchen runs out of food, the chef throws a tantrum when criticized, a rude or lazy waiter, a difficult customer, a customer has forgotten their purse and can't pay, a restaurant is threatened with closure.

Stories

 The Tiger Who Came to Tea by Judith Kerr
Paint big pictures of the tiger and all the food he ate.

 Pumpkin Soup by Helen Cooper
Make some vegetable soup with the children to share at snack time. Act out the story as you stir and season the soup.

 I Will Not Ever Never Eat A Tomato by Lauren Child
Act out situations where children refuse to eat different food.

...one a penny, two a penny, HOT CROSS BUNS!!!

Biscuit Bear by Mini Grey
Write and illustrate new stories about the adventures of Biscuit Bear.

The Lighthouse Keeper's Lunch by Ronda Armitage
Get children to design their own 3D model of a favourite picnic lunch.

Songs and rhymes

- I Like To Eat…
- Food Glorious Food
- Five Currant Buns
- Five Fat Sausages
- Five Fat Peas
- One Potato
- Jelly On The Plate
- Hot Cross Buns
- Polly Put The Kettle On
- Old Tom Tomato
- Pease Pudding Hot
- Pat-A-Cake
- Curly Locks
- Jack Sprat
- Little Jack Horner
- Do You Know The Muffin Man?

Eat Vegetables

(Tune: Aram Sam Sam)
Eat vegetables, eat vegetables,
Eat carrots, peas and broccoli, eat vegetables
Eat vegetables, eat vegetables,
Eat carrots, peas and broccoli, eat vegetables.
Be healthy, be healthy,
Eat carrots, peas and broccoli, eat vegetables.
Be healthy, be healthy,
Eat carrots, peas and broccoli, eat vegetables.

Sandwiches

(Tune: Did You Ever See A Lassie?)
Would you like to make a sandwich,
A sandwich, a sandwich?
Would you like to make a sandwich,
A sandwich with me?
Put some cheese in your sandwich,
Your sandwich, your sandwich.
Put some cheese in your sandwich,
Cheese sandwich for tea.

Change the fillings…

Design, Art and Modelling

Pencils and pens

- *Still life food:* Let children make arrangements of edible objects such as fruit, bread, vegetables, packets, tins and jars. Try sketching using different drawing media.

Paint and print

- *Psychedelic toast:* Paint a design onto a piece of white sliced bread using food colouring mixed with a drop of milk and clean paint brushes. Warn children not to get the bread too wet. Toast and eat!
- *Chocolate pictures:* Paint melted chocolate onto clean sheets of plastic. Leave to dry and then peel off and eat!
- *Biscuit prints:* Choose some hard biscuits with a raised pattern such as Garibaldi or custard creams. Paint ink or dye onto the patterned surface and press onto paper or fabric. Can anyone guess which biscuit has been used?
- *Sticky finger paint:* Mix flour or grains into paint to make a thick finger paint. Spread onto a tabletop, a tray, or thick paper or card, using fingers and hands and create patterns and shapes as a group.
- *Vegetable printing:* Use long carrots, curly cauliflower and round parsnips to create vegetable prints. Invite children

to print them onto a large tureen shape to create an image of vegetable soup.

Collage

- *Favourite meal:* Ask children to cut and stick lots of different collage materials onto a paper plate to create their favourite meal. Try corduroy meat, sponge chips, woolly pasta, bead peas, and shiny paper tomato sauce!
- *Pasta art:* Provide different shapes of pasta to create pictures. Try using long strips of spaghetti for straight lines, and bows, spirals, shells, twists, macaroni, etc.

Modelling

- *Fruit and vegetables:* Scrunch newspaper into different sized balls and tubes. Cover with modroc and shape into apples, oranges, lemons and bananas. Leave to dry and then paint them in their appropriate colours.
- *Mallow creatures:* Use marshmallows and cocktail sticks to build crazy creatures and sculptures.

Clay and dough

- *Model meal:* Use salt and flour dough to create a model meal. Make cylinder sausages, cut out crinkle chips, roll out lots of peas or baked beans! Bake the dough in a very cool oven and then paint and display on paper plates.
- *Time to cook:* Provide lots of different kitchen utensils such as potato masher, forks, spoons, garlic press, rolling pins and let children pretend to cook with the playdough. What food can they create?

Famous Art

Renee Magritte - The son of man
Apple of my eye: Talk about self portraits. Ask children to paint a large self portrait. Cut out a picture of their favourite type of fruit from a magazine and stick on top of the painting!

Roy Lichtenstein - Hot dog
Favourite sandwich Invite children to draw or paint a picture of their favourite sandwich using bold colours.

Dance and Movement

Warm Up

Jelly on a Plate
Perform this song and extend by inviting children to come up with new verses. For example, jelly on my tummy,

jelly on my head, jelly on my toes – wriggling the appropriate body parts as you sing.

Dance

 Children love to dance along to the party song "Pizza Hut".

A Pizza Hut
(form an upside down 'V' with arms above the head)
Kentucky Fried Chicken
(Flap arms like a chicken)
McDonalds
(Form an 'M' with your arms above your head)

Five Currant Buns
Perform the song providing children with props to support their dance

Kitchen Band
Make music using objects usually found in the kitchen – tins, pots and pans, wooden spoons, jars or chopsticks. In a circle or walking around the room create a song or tune all of your own or sing some favourite nursery rhymes.

Movement Games

Find that sound
The children half fill containers such as yoghurt pots with dried foods. You will need at least two of each type of food. Suitable foods could include lentils, dried peas, rice, and pasta or couscous. The containers should be sealed with a secure lid. To start the game, shake one container. The children then try to find the matching sound container. As the children become confident and familiar with the aim of the game you can spread the different containers around the room to encourage movement and increase the challenge.

Cool Down

Imagine it is a warm summer's day and you are having a picnic. Start with a big stretching action as if laying out the blanket. Unpack the hamper. Maybe it needs lifting out of the boot of the car? Encourage the children to describe their actions to you. What food have they bought to the picnic? Have they bought deckchairs that need to be set up? Are there any cheeky ducks you need to chase way as they try to steal your sandwiches? Mime eating your lunch leisurely before settling down for a snooze.

Friends

Drama and Role Play

Drama games

- *Meet and greet:* Ask children to find a space and to then move around, taking care not to bump into anybody. When they hear you call 'meet' they must meet the nearest person and 'greet' them in different ways. Try shaking hands, bowing, hugging, high-fiving, and so on. Vary the type of greeting each time.

Mime

- *Throw that feeling:* Sit in a circle and throw a beanbag to one child. Ask them to then mime a 'feeling' such as sad, happy, scared, angry, excited, worried, calm, tired and so on, just using their face. Then ask them to throw the beanbag on to a friend and call out a different feeling.
- *Friendship chair:* Take turns for two children to sit on a chair in the middle of the circle. Ask them to mime something strange happening to the chair e.g. the chair is burning hot, shrinking, has itching powder or a sharp pin on it, a broken leg, it's too hard, too soft, too small, grows wings and flies away, and so on.

Drama skills

- Use a story, poem or real situation to compose a dramatic argument between two friends. Talk about what can cause arguments. Help children to work in pairs and create an argument. How will they resolve the problem? Remind them that it is only 'pretend'.

Role-play

A playground or park

Set up: Climbing and play equipment, a balance-beam, plastic hoops, balls, quoits, sand pit, bench or seating, an ice-cream van or stall, a pond, sit-and-ride toys, park keeper's hut.

Roles: Children, families, a park keeper.

Stories: Friends are playing at the park: one gets hurt or injured on the equipment; one loses their belonging; they lose each other or an adult; they feed the ducks; find something strange in the park; encounter a grumpy park-keeper. Act out stories from the *Percy the Park Keeper* series by Nick Butterworth.

Stories, Songs and Rhymes

Stories

Lost And Found by Oliver Jeffers
Draw or paint a portrait of your best friend.

Sharing Shell by Julia Donaldson
Create a 3D collage wall display of life in the rock pool with all the different colourful creatures.

Mabel's Magical Garden by Paula Metcalf
Paint comparative pictures of the garden at the beginning of the story and then the garden deprived of sunshine.

The Ugly Duckling Traditional
Act out scenes from the story.

Songs and rhymes

- Polly Put The Kettle On
- Girls And Boys Come Out To Play

Greeting Rhyme
Two best friends, met in a lane,
Hugged each other, and then hugged again,
Said, 'How are you,'
'How are you,'
And 'how are you' again?

Bend thumbs over to greet each other.

My Friend And I
(Tune: Lavender's Blue)
My friend and I
(dilly dilly)
We like to play.
My friend and I
(dilly dilly)
Play all the day
My friend and I
(dilly dilly)

We like to share.
My friend and I
(dilly dilly)
Share cos we care/
Sharing my bear

Making Friends

(Tune: Kumbayah)
Come and share with me
Making friends
Come and share with me
Making friends
Come and share with me
Making friends
Oh _____, be my friend.

Insert name of friend in the gap.

Come and play/read/skip/
swim/eat/etc. with me…

Let's not quarrel now,
Be my friend,
Let's not quarrel now,
Be my friend,
Let's not quarrel now,
Be my friend.
Oh _____, be my friend.

Design, Art and Modelling

Pencils and pens

- *Busy best friends:* Invite children to draw a sketch of their best friend. Draw them doing their favourite activity such as playing football, painting, eating, building with bricks, playing with cars, dancing, etc.

Paint and print

- *Symmetrical art:* Ask children to work with a friend. Divide a piece of paper in half. One child paints a picture on one half and then invites a friend to paint an exact copy or mirror image on the other side of the paper.
- *Friendly portraits* Ask children to place a big piece of paper on an easel and ask a friend to pose for a portrait. Make a posh frame using cardboard, pasta shapes and gold or silver spray paint.

Collage

- *Photo fits:* Make a photo fit picture of a friend's face using collage materials and cut out shapes. Try cutting out different features from magazines. Can the children recognise themselves? Display alongside actual photographs of children.

Modelling

- *Paper pals:* Make a model friend using newspaper. Twist and fold the paper into a body shape. Add limbs and attach with masking tape. Use a wooden posable figure as a guide.
- *Friendship bracelets:* Make paper beads from strips of magazine paper, spread with glue and wrapped around a plastic straw. Leave them to dry and cut into beads. Thread onto string or elastic to make a bracelet or necklace for a friend.

Clay and dough

- *Firm friends:* Make a clay model of a friend's face. Roll out the clay to a thickness of 5mm and then cut out a circle or oval shape. Use tools to cut the eye shapes. Add shaped lumps of clay for the nose, lips and ears. Use a garlic press to squeeze the clay into strands of hair and arrange on the face.

Famous Art

Mabel Lucy Atwell - Illustrations of

children playing together

Me and my mate: Cut out pictures of children playing from greetings cards. Stick two together on a paper plate and then cover in glue as a varnish. Leave to dry. Let children share a snack together with a friend.

Dance and Movement

Warm Up

Climb into an imaginary boat with a friend to perform this adaptation of the traditional rhyme Row Row Row Your Boat.

Love love love your friends
Love them all year long
Especially on this special day as we sing this song

In a circle perform this adaptation of Ring a Ring a Roses.

Ring a ring a roses, a pocket full of posies
Atichoo atichoo we all fall down
Lots of love and kisses from all of us and me
We all jump up with a one two three

Dance

Take your partners
Invite the children to get into pairs to free dance to a piece of popular music – ideally a love song. Children particularly enjoy songs from their favourite movies. Adults can encourage children by showing them how to twirl their partners or how to move around in circles. Don't worry if children get into threes or fours; it often happens and adds to the fun!

This is a wonderful activity for everyone to build relationships and trust, including adults. Have some snuggle time. Immobile children can be held and rocked to the music.

Dancing with Balloons
Give the children red, white and pink balloons. Let them free dance with the balloons encouraging them to jump with, kick, throw and catch the balloons. Background music can be lively or peaceful depending on the mood of the children or how loud you want the activity to be.

Movement Games

I wrote a letter to my friend.
Play as you would I wrote a letter to my love. Before starting the game ask the children to decorate a large envelope that can then be used for the game prop.

Cool Down

(To the tune of If you're happy and you know it)

If you love me and you know it blow a kiss
If you love me and you know it give a hug
If you love me and you know it sing "you're my friend"
Can the children create actions to match each verse? How many other verses can the children come up with? Can you perform it whispering?

Gardens

Drama and Role Play

Drama games

- *I went to the garden:* Use the well-known rhyme to act out planting and watering plants, and getting rid of pests, as you grow plants in the garden.
- *Lists:* This is a word game that can be adapted to lots of different topics. Go round the circle naming different flowers and plants from the garden. Take care not to repeat one already named.

Mime

- Choose three or four different activities that might happen in a garden such as: playing in a paddling pool, weeding the flower bed, mowing the lawn, playing on the swing, playing hide and seek. Ask children to mime each of them and change quickly between them when you call out the instructions.

Drama skills

- Improvise a drama about someone who needs help in their garden. Go into role as an old person and describe your garden: the long grass, lots of weeds, a broken fence, huge stones in the soil etc. Organise the children into three or four groups and get them to help with each of the problems. How will they get rid of the stones? Will they build a wall or rockery, move them in a wheelbarrow or bury them. Work with the children's ideas. Add tension by saying the work has to be completed before it rains.
- Act out the story of *Jasper's Beanstalk* by Nick Butterworth as Jasper tries to grow a plant and instead grows more and more impatient. Compare this with the traditional story of Jack and the Beanstalk.

Role-play

The garden centre
Set up: Real and pretend plants, tools, flowers, shopping baskets, plant pots, watering cans, seed packets, garden furniture, sand, gravel, buckets, wheelbarrows, aprons, gardening gloves, boots. Make your own seed packets using cut-out pictures from seed catalogues and sealed envelopes full of rice.

Roles: Manager, shop keepers, customers, gardeners.

Stories: A very busy shop with not enough staff; a naughty dog loose in the store; flowers and plants start dying mysteriously; a wheel falls off a wheelbarrow, and so on.

Stories, Songs and Rhymes

Stories

- *Jasper's Beanstalk* by Nick Butterworth
Use either a days of the week rhyme such as 'Solomon Grundy' or use rhymes below to create your own rhyme about Jasper's attempts to grow a plant.

- *Oliver's Vegetables* by Vivian French
Act out the story as Oliver learns to try different vegetables from granddad's garden.

Eddie's Garden by Sarah Garland
Use ICT, draw or paint a design of your own garden.

The Global Garden by Kate Petty
Create a visual aid using flaps and wheels from the book
to share information about plants from around the world.

Songs and rhymes

- I Went to the Garden and Dug up the Ground
- Mary Mary Quite Contrary
- Sing a Song of Sixpence

The Vegetables are Growing

(Tune: John Brown's body)
The vegetables are growing
In my garden, in a line.
The vegetables are growing
In my garden, now it's fine.
The vegetables are growing
In my garden, all the time.
Let's count them carefully.
Can you count the orange carrots?
Can you count the tasty spinach?
Can you count the new potatoes?
Growing in the ground.

A Week In The Garden

On Monday I planted the seed.
On Tuesday I pulled out a weed.
On Wednesday I watered the ground.
On Thursday I walked all around.
On Friday I began to doubt.
On Saturday I pulled the seed out!
On Sunday I did what I do best.
Sat in my garden having a rest!

Pencils and pens

- *Patio art:* Draw a frame on an outdoor surface using chalk. Use chalks and pastels to create a work of art inside the frame.
- *Greenery:* Fold a piece of paper into quarters to form rectangles. Use a range of green pencils and wax crayons. Draw and make marks in each section, experimenting to show the texture of grasses, the underside of a leaf and stems, etc.

Paint and print

- *Flowerpots:* Use clean clay or plastic flowerpots and acrylic paints. Decorate the pots using garden images and patterns.
- *Garden printing:* Encourage children to collect and bring in a variety of objects from their garden. Use leaves, conkers, seeds and twigs, etc. to dip into paint and use as tools to create a picture.

Collage

- *Cuttings and clippings:* Create collage gardens using cut outs from seed catalogues, corrugated card, lolly sticks, netting, flowery material, etc. Arrange chosen cuttings and other materials to make a garden. Will it have a shed, fence, path, rockery, water feature, toys, etc.?
- *Weaving:* Use a large piece of garden netting and hang up outdoors. Provide a variety of ribbons, silks, fabrics and wool and experiment with weaving the materials in and out of the netting. Tie on shiny foil shapes, button and bows.

Modelling

- *Weeping willows:* Provide a range of papers and card cut into strips and a variety of lengths. Experiment with rolling, fringing, folding and tearing the strips to make hanging leaves. Help children to attach both ends of each strip to a large piece of card with tape. Work as a group to attach more leaf strips weaving them in and out, over and under previous leaves.
- *Design a garden:* Line a shallow foil tray with moss, and fill with stones, soil, film containers with small cut flowers, small plants and quick growing seeds to create a living work of art!

Clay and dough

- *Coil flowerpot:* Roll clay into long sausage-shaped lengths. Cut out a circle and smooth the beginning of one length onto the circular base. Coil the length of clay round and then add another building it up into a simple coil pot. Smooth the outside coils to fix, fire or air dry and decorate.

Famous Art

Claude Monet – Iris Garden at Giverny

Pastel garden: Use chunky pastels and chalks to make a copy of this colourful garden. Include, trees, branches, flowers and a path.

Dance and Movement

Warm Up

Children pretend to be something often found in a garden – maybe a tree, some long grass or washing drying on the line. Imagine a breeze flowing through the garden – how might they move? The breeze grows into a strong wind. Encourage the children to describe their actions and movements to each other and you.

Dance

Parachute Dance

Holding the edges of the parachute walk, skip, hop or jump round in a circle singing Ring a Roses. As you sing, "Fishes in the water, fishes in the sea" make waves with the parachute. Round and Round the Garden. When you sing "Tickly under there" children run under the parachute screaming or giggling. Alternatively sing "one step, two step and shake it all about" then shake the parachute.

Fairies & Pixies

Tell the children you are going on a trip to the bottom of the garden where you will all become fairies and pixies. Use the music of Edvard Greig "In the Hall of the Mountain King" to inspire children's movement and performance. This chant is a good way to start the dance;

Down at the bottom of the garden
Where no one else can see
There lives a family of fairies and pixies
They always welcome me

Movement Games

 A wriggly race

Children make believe they are a creepy crawly. Starting at one end of the garden they wriggle and slime their way to a finish post. You can vary the race by doing it backwards or introducing obstacles such as plant pots and watering cans for them to manoeuvre around.

Cool Down

Mary Mary Quite Contrary.

Children take it in turns to play the part of Mary and perform actions to suit the song while the others sing. If it is a large group break up the children into smaller groups to make sure all children have a turn at playing Mary and to help ensure this is a calm and quiet activity.

Growth

introduce change as they begin to grow shoots and grow up into a plant with flowers, or a tall tree. Make all the movements tiny and very slow, as that is more challenging. Use slow, changing music to help with the concentration.

- *What's my line going to be?:* Talk about what jobs the children would like to do when they grow up. Ask them to mime the job for the others to guess. See also the topics of Ourselves and Night.

Drama skills

- *Jack and the Beanstalk:* Retell the traditional story. Talk about the different characters : Jack, Jack's mum, the cow, the bean seller, the giant and the giant's wife. Divide the story into scenes and act out the story. Interview characters from the story. How did Jack's mum feel when he brought home a handful of beans? How did the giant's wife feel when Jack came back the second time? Was the giant really bad or was he just protecting his property? Who was the mysterious bean seller?

Role-play

The giant's castle

Set up: Oversized furniture and adult clothes. A bag of coins, a soft-toy hen, a miniature harp made from cardboard and strings. Lots of places to hide.

Roles: Jack, giant, giant's wife.

Stories: Jack and the beanstalk, hide and seek, the adventures of the giant before Jack came to visit. Where did the giant get the magic hen from?

Drama and Role Play

Drama games

- *Breathing:* Ask children to stand up straight and practice breathing in and out. Ask them to breathe in to the count of 3, hold their breath for 3 and then breathe out. Make sure they don't lift their shoulders. When they are confident with this ask them to breathe out through different lip shapes such as 'oo', 'ah' and 'ee'. Lengthen the time that children hold their breath to the count of 5 and then 10.

Mime

- Try some physical drama about a growing seed. Ask children to curl up small like a seed. Very slowly

Stories, Songs and Rhymes

Stories

Jack and the Beanstalk Traditional
Explore pitch, i.e. high and low sounds, using a xylophone or keyboard. Increase the pitch as the beanstalk grows taller.

The Tiny Seed by Eric Carle
Copy the book's unique style of art by tearing paper of different colours to create a collage of flowers.

The Enormous Turnip Traditional
Act out the story.

Once there were Giants by Martin Waddell
Draw a picture of what each child wants to be when grown up.

Songs and rhymes

- Mary Mary Quite Contrary
- I Went To The Garden And Dug Up The Ground
- Five Fat Peas In A Peapod Pressed
- 'Now I Am Six' by A.A.Milne
- Oats And Beans And Barley Grow
- I Had A Little Nut Tree
- Once I Found A Cherry Stone

I Grow Best While I'm Asleep

I grow best while I'm asleep,
Out from the covers my toes will peep.
My hair will grow, my fingers too,
I'm still growing, how about you?

And That's Not All!

When I was a baby
I couldn't even walk.
When I was a baby
I couldn't even talk.
Now I am five
I've grown very tall.
I can run and skip and jump
And that's not all!
I can sing and shout out loud
And that's not all!
I can read and write my name
And that's not all!

(Add own achievements?)

Down In The Garden
(Tune: Down In The Jungle)
Down in the garden
Where nobody goes,
I planted a seed
To watch it grow.
I watered it here,
I watered it there,
I watered it just about everywhere!

It grew very, very tall
It grew very, very tall

It grew very, very tall
It grew just about everywhere!

Pencils and pens

- *Plant diary:* Keep a plant diary showing the growth from seed to flower and draw pictures of each stage. Add photographs.
- *Growing smaller:* Play with a Russian doll and separate out all the figures. Draw pictures of the dolls in a line as they grow smaller and smaller.

Paint and print

- *As time goes by:* Ask children to bring in baby photographs. Can they recognise each other as babies? Paint two-part portraits of themselves as a baby and 'now'.
- *Paint blots:* Mix some food colouring with water and place in a small bowl. Fold a piece of kitchen towel in half and then half again. Dip each corner into the dye and watch the colour spread or grow up the paper. Repeat by refolding and adding a different colour.

Collage

- *Living art:* In a shallow plastic tray, arrange some damp cotton wool and sprinkle mustard and cress seeds in a pattern. Try a simple shape such as a circle or a letter or a more complex pattern. The seeds should grow into a living work of art!

- *Bean mosaic:* Make a collection of different-sized dried beans and create a mosaic pattern or picture.

Modelling

- *Flowerpots:* Make a collection of different-sized plastic flowerpots. Stuff with shredded green or brown tissue paper. Add a long straw stem and a flower head (see templates at the back of this book) using tissue paper, cardboard, felt, etc. Decorate with beads, buttons and sequins.

Clay and dough

- *Growing worms:* Take balls of playdough or plasticine and roll them into sausages. Challenge children to make either the longest or thinnest worm.

Famous Art

Georgia O'Keeffe
- Magnified flower paintings

Gigantic blooms: Use crayons, pastels or paint to create giant close up pictures of flowers.

Warm Up

Sort the group by height standing children and adults in a row to show the tallest to the smallest. Repeat this by kneeling, crouching or sitting.

Dance

♫ Babies to Giants
Invite children to dance as a baby might, crawling, wiggling and babbling along to the music. Progress to dancing like children, moving onto adults – how does Mummy or Daddy dance? Can they dance like their grandparents or even a giant?

What type of dancer do you want to be when you're older? Provide different styles of dance music for the children to explore – ballroom, Latin, salsa, ballet, and jive and so on. Providing suitable dressing up clothes will enhance this dance further.

♫ Dance along to the children's classic "Them Bones Them Bones" found on many children's CDs.

Movement Games

✎ Big Box Little Box
With the children place a small box inside a slightly larger box and then place those into another slightly larger box. Keep going with as many boxes as you want until you have a "Russian Doll" style pass the parcel. Sit down or stand up to play pass the parcel with your boxes. Extend this game by placing "dancing forfeits" inside each box. Forfeits can include:

HOP ON ONE LEG
DO AN IRISH JIG
DANCE A SILLY DANCE
DO THE CAN CAN

🎭 Jumping Beans
Use actions such as;

- Daddy (stand with arms stretched up tall)
- Mummy (pretend to push a pram around)
- Baby (pretend to rock a baby in your arms)
- Brother (pretend to be playing football)

Before starting the game, request ideas for actions from the children.

Cool Down

🎭 You will need some background music that is calming and if possible represents the outdoors or weather. Imagine you are leaves on a tree. As the wind blows you break free and get caught up in the wind gently blowing around on the breeze. Ask the children to think about how a leaf moves – gracefully gliding. Finally settle on the ground and lie down under the shade of the tree.

Holes

Drama games

- *The answer is..:* This is a great game for trying to keep a straight face, which children really enjoy. Choose a word such as 'doughnuts' and agree that whatever question you ask the answer must be 'doughnuts'. Then ask questions such as 'what do you wear to go to bed?' and 'what is your brother's name?'

Mime

- *Mime different ways of moving through a hole:* 'hide in a hole' – curl up small and then emerge slowly out of the hole; 'stuck in a hole' – pretend to be crawling through a hole and get stuck; 'fall in a hole' – mime falling into a hole; 'lost in a hole' – go through the hole and pretend to get lost. What is in the hole?
- *Pass the holey prop:* Sit in a circle and pass round a prop such as a hoop, ring, hair bobble or loop of string. Ask the children to mime using the 'holey' prop in different ways. Can the others guess what they are pretending it is?

Drama skills

- Use hoops to represent entrances to holes. As the children climb through they find themselves somewhere else. Ask them to make up where they are. Just choose one thing to start with that has changed such as temperature, time of day, mood etc. Then extend the improvisation and use as the start of a fantasy story.

Role-play

Animal hole or burrow

Set up: Make a dark area using drapes with a play-tunnel to crawl through as the entrance. Use some home corner furniture and props to create an animal home in the hole.

Roles: Animals such as rabbits, badgers, moles, foxes etc.

Stories: A new hole to furnish and clean; hold a 'hole warming party' in the hole; the animals home is under threat from the farmer or building work etc.

Stories

Peepo! by Janet and Allan Ahlberg
Paint or draw a picture of a baby's or child's activities and then place a piece of paper on top with a hole cut out in the style of the book.

Another Fine Mess by Tony Bonning
Use junk materials and empty food packets to create pictures from the story.

Wait Until Dinnertime by Mel Astill
Add sound effects to the story below using voices, body percussion and musical instruments.

Wait until Dinnertime

Baby Rabbit was hungry. "You're always hungry", said Mummy Rabbit, "wait until dinnertime!" Baby Rabbit leapt out of his

burrow hole. "Mmmm", he thought, "what can I eat?" He hopped into the next burrow hole and found some delicious carrots that Grandad Rabbit was saving for breakfast. "Mmmm, crunchy", he said as he munched.

Baby Rabbit climbed through the next burrow hole and found some crisp, green lettuce leaves that Uncle Rabbit was saving for lunch. "Mmmm, lovely", he said as he munched.

Baby Rabbit squeezed into the next burrow hole and found some fresh dandelions that cousin rabbit was saving for dinner. "Mmmm, tasty", he said as he munched.

Baby Rabbit felt rather full and tired after all that eating. He peered out of the burrow hole, it was getting dark. "Dinnertime", he could hear Mummy Rabbit calling. "I must get back to my burrow," he said. But oh dear, Baby Rabbit was stuck. His tummy was too big and too full and the hole was too small. He pushed and squeezed but it was no good.

"Mummy, I'm stuck!" he cried. Mummy Rabbit took his paws and heaved and pulled and eventually out popped Baby Rabbit. "Next time I think you should wait until dinnertime!" said mummy.

Songs and rhymes

- There's A Hole In My Bucket
- Put Your Finger In Foxy's Hole

Make Me A Doughnut
(Tune: Pat-A-Cake)
Pat-a-cake, pat-a-cake, baker's man,
Bake me a doughnut, as fast as you can.
Mix it and shape it, and roll in a ring,
Make me a doughnut that's fit for a king!

Make A Hole
(Tune: Oh We Can Play On The Big Bass Drum)
Can you make a hole with your fingers?
And this is the way you do it.
Make a hole with your fingers and thumb
And then you can look right through it.

Can you make a hole with both your hands?
And this is the way you do it.
Join your fingers and join your thumbs
And then you can look right through it.

Design, Art and Modelling

Pencils and pens

- *Stencils:* Use cut out sheets from new board games as stencils. Draw inside the shaped holes and crayon in different colours.

Paint and print

- *Punchinella paints:* Provide strips and squares of punchinella or sequin waste. Tape securely to paper and then paint over the holes using a roller or brush to create holey patterns.
- *Sponge roller:* Help children to cut different sizes and shapes of holes into a thin sheet of sponge. Stick the sheet of sponge around a paint roller. Roll in paint and then on paper to make holes appear. Which is the biggest or smallest hole?

Collage

- *Punch it, stick it:* Provide a range of hole punchers and punch holes from a variety of papers and card. Create a hole punched collage by arranging holey paper onto a large sheet of paper and sticking down. Add the paper cut from the holes to make a contrasting picture.

Modelling

- *Pencil pots:* Cut three different lengths of cardboard tube and stick together in an upright position on a cardboard or plastic base. Cover in paper or paint to decorate.

Clay and dough

- *Hedgehog pencil block:* Make a lump of clay into an interesting shape and use a blunt pencil to make 5 or 6 deep holes. Decorate around the edges using clay tools and leave to dry. Place a pencil or pen in each hole.

Famous Art

Dame Barbara Hepworth – Two Figures (1964)

Create and cut out: Talk about the sculpture: what shapes can the children see? How has it been made? Use plasticine or playdough to create similar forms to those in the sculpture. Cut out holes using clay tools. What can the children see through the holes in their sculpture?

Dance and Movement

Warm Up

 Using a pop-up tunnel, invite children to move through it in as many different ways as they can think

of. Maybe they want to crawl through it, or slide on their tummies or even go backwards!

Dance

Hula Hoops
Give the children hula hoops (of different colours and sizes if possible). In a clear open space let them dance and play with the equipment. Provide lively fun background music to enhance the dance.

Heigh- Ho
Using the "Heigh- Ho" track from Disney's Snow White, encourage children to dance along as the seven dwarfs working in the tunnels of the diamond mine. Providing appropriate props such as hard hats, torches and pretend tools will add to the experience.

Movement Games

There's a hole in my bucket
The children form teams and stand at one end of the playground or garden. Place a paddling pool or large container at the opposite end (one for each team). Each team is given a bucket with a hole in it and identical large containers of water. The children take it in turns to fill their bucket and run to the opposite end to empty it into their paddling pool. The aim is to transport as much of their team's water from one end to the other end as quickly as possible. Great fun on a sunny day. Before starting the game the children may enjoy colouring their water with paint, food colouring or glitter. Add another by adding food colouring with a distinctive smell such as vanilla or peppermint essence.

Cool Down

Give each child a coit. Standing calmly, hold the coit in your hands and invite children to perform slow controlled movements;

Stretch up tall
Stretch to the right and then the left
Make circles in the air
Encourage children's suggestions for movements.

Holidays

Drama games

- *Beachcombing:* Pass items around the circle found on the beach and ask children to pretend they are something else. A shell becomes a hat or a mobile phone, a piece of wood is shaped like a knife, the seaweed becomes a brush for sweeping the floor. How many different uses can the children invent for each item?
- *Hot seats:* Invite children to talk for half a minute about a favourite holiday. Record or film their efforts. This is a good game for developing children's confidence in speaking to a group. Ask the children to choose alternative subjects to talk about.

Mime

- *A walk in the sand:* Mime walking on different surfaces and move appropriately. For example soft sand – slippery, feet sink into the sand; hot sand – starts to get hot from the sun, take small quick steps on tip-toes to avoid being burned; pebbles – difficult to walk on, hurt feet, and fall over; rocks – clamber over the spikey shapes, and scratch or cut feet; wet sand – draw a picture or write your name with your toes.

Drama skills

- Go on a journey to the beach. Act out the sequence of events involved. Pile into the car with lots of equipment. Find a good place to sit or set up camp. Apply suntan cream, change and go for a swim in the sea. What if the water is cold? Eat picnic food and read a book. Build a sandcastle, go fishing in the rock pools, eat an ice-cream. As the sun goes down, pack up and go home.

Role-play

A travel agents
Set up: Tables and chairs, telephones, computer screens, diaries, lots of holiday brochures and posters, tickets, passports.

Roles: Travel agents, customers.

Stories: Organising a dream holiday; holiday-makers come in to complain very loudly; a rude customer on the phone keeps interrupting, and so on.

Stories

 Mr Bear's Holiday by Debi Gliori
Design a fancy patterned tent to rival Mr. Bear's.

Lisa's Airplane Trip by Anne Gutman
Act out Lisa's adventures on her first experience on a plane.

 The Cat Who Wanted To Go Home by Jill Tomlinson
Use balloons, papier mache and paint to create model hot-air balloons.

 Holiday Day by Mel Astill
Paint a picture of a perfect holiday day.

Holiday Day

Martha wanted to go on holiday. On a holiday with sun for bathing in, waves for splashing in, sand for building with and lots of ice cream for licking. But.... mum and dad were always busy at work and that meant no holiday for Martha.

One Saturday, Martha woke up, and discovered it was sunny and hot, the perfect day for a holiday. "Oh I wish I had waves to splash in, sand to build with and even just one ice-cream to lick would be nice," thought Martha. She went downstairs to have breakfast. Where were mum and dad? Busy as usual, thought Martha grumpily.

She called out, no answer. She called again and listened.... she could hear laughing and splashing sounds in the garden. Martha ran outside. Mum and dad had been busy. The paddling pool was full with cool, sparkling water. The sand pit was full with bright yellow sand for building castles, and there was even a beach towel for bathing in the sun. It WAS going to be the most perfect holiday day!

"Now then," said mum, "time for breakfast! What will it be: toast, cornflakes, porridge or....an ice cream for licking?"

Can you guess what Martha chose?

Songs and rhymes

- We're all going on a summer holiday

On my holiday
(Tune: Jelly on the plate)
On my holiday
On my holiday
Building castles
Building castles
Lots of games to play.

On my holiday
On my holiday
Fill the bucket
Fill the bucket
Lots of games
to play.

Other verses could include these choruses: turn it over, hoist the flag, have a paddle, waves are coming, now the castle's gone!

Design, Art and Modelling

Pencils and pens

- *Sketch-a-suitcase:* Provide a simple suitcase template (see templates at the back of this book) and cut out using coloured paper. Draw items to 'pack 'into the case: a bucket, a spade, swimming trunks, teddy bear, etc.

- *Wet sand art:* Draw pictures, shapes and patterns in wet sand using hands, feet and different tools.

Paint and print

- *Pebble pals:* Provide a variety of pebbles, paint, pva glue and adhesive 'googly' eyes. Paint the pebbles and leave to dry. Seal with pva and add the eyes. Ask children to name their pebble pals?
- *Combing:* Paint a wavescape using green, blue and white paint. Make a comb with stiff card and/or use real combs. Apply paints from squeezy bottles to one side of a piece of paper and use the combs to make the waves flow across.

Collage

- *Beach art:* Make big pictures using sand, shells, seaweed, pebbles, driftwood, etc. Photograph to record.
- *North American Indian sand art:* Provide sand coloured with powder paint. Draw a simple picture using thick black felt pen and cover each section in glue. Sprinkle different coloured sand onto each section using spoons, fingers or cones.

Modelling

- *Holiday treats:* Make simple cones from thin card and add scrunched up tissue paper ice cream. Apply toppings using squeezy paints, sequins and foam shapes. Try painting cardboard tubes in bright colours and wrap in cellophane to make sticks of rock.

Clay and dough

● *Pressed pebbles:* Roll out large shapes of playdough or plasticine. Use pebbles and shells, seaweed and drift wood to make marks and patterns.

Famous Art

George Pierre Seurat – Bathers at Asnieres

Holiday sketches: Look at the painting and talk about the different activities: swimming, sunbathing, etc. Ask children to bring in a photo of themselves on holiday (at home or away). Ask them to draw themselves on the beach, at the park, swimming, playing or maybe even sunbathing!

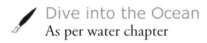

Dance and Movement

Warm Up

 Imagine packing a large suitcase to take on holiday. Exaggerating all movements, open the case, select clothes and fold them neatly, perhaps there is too much in your case and you struggle to close it, carry it to the car and load it into the boot.

Dance

♫ We're all going on a summer holiday

Dance along to this popular song. Enhance the dance by providing children with appropriate props. You may like to choose props themed towards different types of holidays such as camping, caravanning or a beach holiday.

Paradise Island

Invite children to move like the things found on a tropical beach;

The waves of the sea
The swaying palm trees
The flying birds
The scurrying crabs
The swimming fish
Encourage children's own suggestions. Provide aquatic sounding music to give added atmosphere.

♫ Adventure

Imagine you are the animals on an African safari. Encourage children to think of the animals they might find and how they might move about. Allow children

the opportunity to dance and perform as their animals. Providing traditional African music will enhance the activity. Alternatively imagine you are in the jungle with jungle animals and music.

Movement games

Holiday Clothes

Scatter holiday clothes around the room and invite children to race to fill an empty suitcase with the items. Alternatively give children a pile of holiday clothes and let them race against the clock or each other to dress up ready for their holidays!

Dive into the Ocean

As per water chapter

Cool Down

Sit the group in a circle leaving a large space between each person. In doing this you are ensuring children will need to stretch in order to reach each other. Then pass different holiday related object around; beach balls, rubber rings, shells, hats and so on. To achieve further stretches repeat standing up or lying down.

Houses and Homes

Drama games

- *Four corners:* Talk about different sorts of homes that animals live in. Choose four types of animals' homes such as a nest, burrow, hole in a tree, or cave and draw or label the four corners of the room. Ask all the children to move around the room until you call out the name of an animal, such as a sparrow, squirrel, rabbit, badger, bee, bat, bear, etc. The children must then choose which home to run to.

Mime

- *This is the house that Jack built:* Use this rhyme to mime building a house together.
- *Who's that at the door?:* Ask for a volunteer to come and knock on the door, then come in the room and mime a character for the others to guess. Use dressing-up clothes and props to develop mimes.

Drama skills

- *The Three Little Pigs:* Retell the traditional story. Divide into scenes and act out the story. Talk about the characters of the three little pigs. How could they vary from each other? Introduce 'hot seating', i.e. speaking and answering as if they were a character in the story. Rewrite the ending.
- *The haunted house:* Improvise a drama about a haunted house. Introduce characters that are brave, lazy, scared, bossy, and small. They dare each other to visit the big, empty house and hear lots of strange sounds. How do the different characters react?

Role-play

Estate agents

Set up: Tables and chairs, computers, telephones, house details, local newspapers, a diary, bunches of keys.

Roles: Manager, estate agents, customers: both buyers and sellers.

Stories: Visit a house that is not for sale by mistake; be late for an appointment; encounter a very fussy or angry customer; the house is falling down, and so on.

Stories

The Three Little Pigs Traditional
Act out the story.

The Three Liitle Wolves And The Big Bad Pig
by Eugene Trivizas
Use a range of materials to create a model-house that the three little pigs couldn't demolish!

Hansel and Gretel Tradtional
Create a giant collage picture of a house made of all the children's favourite sweets using wrappers and labels.

The Little, Little House by Jessica Souhami
Cut paper shapes in the style of the artwork to create
a picture of a house bursting at the seams.

Songs and rhymes

- I'm Going To Build A Little House
- How many people live in your house?
- This Is The House That Jack Built
- Peter Hammers With One Hammer
- There Was A Crooked Man
- To Market, To Market

Made Into A Home
(Tune: The Wheels On The Bus)
My house is built of big red bricks,
Big red bricks, big red bricks,
My house is built of big red bricks,
Made into a home.

My house is built with four wide windows,
Four wide windows, four wide windows,
My house is built with four wide windows,
Made into a home.

*Make up new verses using these ideas: a tiled roof, a 'red' front
door, a garden wall, a long green garage etc.*

Jason Builds
(Tune; Peter Hammers)
Jason builds with one brick,
One brick, one brick.
Jason builds with one brick
All day long.
Sally builds with two bricks…

*Build up the rhyme using the names of all children, then count
back down again.*

Design, Art and Modelling

Pencils and pens

- *Rub it!:* Take a walk with the children to look for a
  variety of bricks, manhole covers, fences and interesting
  raised surfaces. Place paper over each surface and make
  rubbings using wax crayons held lengthways.
- *Home:* Ask children to draw a picture of their home.
  What colour is the door? What shape are the windows?
  Is there a front garden?

Paint and print

- *Window painting:* Help children to make a window
  using a laminator pouch or a piece of transparent
  shower curtain. Paint a view on the window. Will it be
  a landscape or cityscape? Leave to dry and then apply a
  painted frame. Hang up in the window.
- *Printed places:* Print shapes using a variety of shaped
  sponges, wooden and duplo bricks. Combine the shapes
  to make a printed home. Will it be a house, a block of
  flats, a cottage, or even a castle?

Collage

- *Wallpaper design:* Make a collection of wallpapers. What
  patterns are on them? Which rooms might they be
  used in? Arrange wallpaper cut outs, pre-cut shapes and
  child's own shapes to create a new wallpaper.
- *Skyline:* Cut out shapes of houses and buildings in black
  paper and create a skyline silhouette. Stick onto backing
  paper painted with sunset stripes of blue, red, orange
  and yellow.

Modelling

- *Junk model buildings:* Use boxes and packets to make
  different model homes and buildings. Cut out windows

and doors. Add a sloping roof and a chimney or two. Paint and layout on a street map or hillside.

Clay and dough

- *Birds nest:* Add sticks and twigs to playdough or plasticine and build a birds nest. Add some marbled rolled eggs.
- *Bear cave:* Make a model cave from clay for some toy bears to hibernate in. Which other animal homes could children build using clay?

Famous Art

Friedensreich Hundertwasser - Vienna Houses

Toppling tower blocks: Use photographs or images of architecture as a starting point for drawings. Use long rectangular paper, pencils, pens and a range of 2D shape templates (see templates at the back of this book). Draw round the shapes and experiment with making Hundertwasser houses!

Dance and Movement

Warm Up

 Try these actions slowly and exaggerated. Stretch up tall like a chimney, arms and legs out wide like a house. Climb the stairs. Open and close the door or curtains. Bend down low to touch the floor. Can the children think of any other actions?

Dance

Tidy up Time

Invite the children to imagine they are cleaning their homes or bedroom. Provide props to encourage dance; mops, brooms and dusters are great. Provide lively background music to encourage movement.

If you're happy and you know it clean the house
If you're happy and you know it mop the floor
If you're happy and you know it clean the windows
If you're happy and you know it scrub the bath

 Stand up to perform this song. Invite the children to make up appropriate actions to match the verses. Encourage the children to think up new verses.

Dance along to the "Mambo Number Five" by Bob the Builder. Create actions to match the lyrics.

Movement Games

Musical houses

Give the children cardboard boxes and suitable creative materials to decorate as houses. Once complete spread the boxes out in a clear open space. Alternatively give the children sheets and chairs or tables to create tents and wigwams. Children dance around the houses while music is played. When the music stops children must jump into the nearest house/ tent/ wigwam.

Cool Down

Imagine you are bears returning to your cave for a peaceful rest. Alternatives – a rabbit returning to the burrow, a bird returning to a nest, a cat returning to a basket. Can the children think of any more? Play peaceful calming music whilst the children perform.

Journeys

Drama and Role Play

Drama games

- *In my shoes:* Make a collection of different types of shoes. Put them in the middle of the circle and invite children to try them on and assume the character of someone who would wear them. Ask them to invent a line of dialogue to introduce their character. Can they go on an appropriate journey? For instance if they choose Wellington boots they can pretend to be a gardener walking round his garden, or ballet slippers a dancer who is late for a performance.

Mime

- *Follow my leader:* Play follow my leader games around the room. Make the path change between straight, bendy, and sharp turns. Vary the levels at which children move by asking them to dip under branches, crawl through tunnels and climb up hills, over stiles and other obstacles. Walk alongside streams, wade through water and balance across bridges.
- *Magic carpet:* See the topic of Flight.

Drama skills

- *Journey dilemmas:* Improvise journeys and introduce dilemmas or problems for the children to solve such as: getting lost, being late for an important date, forgetting something important, leaving someone behind, getting stuck in a traffic jam, a cancelled train or a car accident.

Role-play

A garage

Set up: Sit-and-ride vehicles, tools, overalls, spare parts and tyres, a petrol pump made from a painted cardboard box with dials and a hose, a radio, cash till, car magazines, a telephone. Set up a garage shop with newspapers, flowers and confectionary. Provide props for the car wash: buckets, sponges, shammy leathers, hoses etc. Build a breakdown truck and use a tow rope to rescue broken-down vehicles.

Roles: Manager, mechanics, petrol-pump attendant, salesperson, customers etc.

Stories: The car is not ready on time for the customer; there is trouble mending the car; the garage runs out of petrol; a customer's car is scratched; a rude customer, and so on.

Stories, Songs and Rhymes

Stories

The Train Ride by June Crebbin
Recite the story rhythmically as a chant and add sound effects for the different things the train passes on its journey.

We All Go Traveling By by Sheena Roberts
Sing along to the accompanying CD and have fun creating sound effects.

The Snail and the Whale by Julia Donaldson
Draw and paint pictures of maps of the snail's journey.

Hansel and Gretel Traditional
Act out the story of the children's journey through the forest, following a trail.

Songs and rhymes

- The Wheels On The Bus
- Row Row Row The Boat
- Ride A Cock Horse

Visiting
(Tune: I went to visit a farm one day)
We went to visit the/a _____ one day
We'll see a _____ along the way
What d'ya think we'll hear it say?

Fill in the gaps with appropriate words such as friend/house/shop/ farm/park/zoo/sea etc.

Travelling Rap
(Echo each line)
Open the gate
Don't be late
Get in the car
Don't go far
Down the road
Watch the load
Round the bend
Towards the end
Going fast
Can't be last
Slowing down
Into town
Come to a stop
That's your lot!

I'm On A Journey
(Tune: Ants go marching)
My feet go marching two by two, Hurrah, hurrah,
My feet go marching two by two,
Hurrah, hurrah,
My feet go marching two by two,
They're marching round to come see you
And I'm on a journey, traveling along.

My car is driving very fast,
Hurrah, hurrah,
My car is driving very fast,
Hurrah, hurrah,
My car is driving very fast,
Its driving fast, it won't be last,
And I'm on a journey, traveling along.

The train is whizzing quickly by,
Hurrah, hurrah,
The train is whizzing quickly by,
Hurrah, hurrah,
The train is whizzing quickly by,
Look out the window as we fly,
And I'm on a journey, traveling along.

Design, Art and Modelling

Pencils and pens

- *Wheel crazy:* Study different shapes and sizes of wheels. Compare the curved lines for tyres and straight lines for spokes? Provide a range of drawing media, e.g. silver and gold wax crayons, pens, felt tips and different sizes of circle templates. Create a group masterpiece of wheels using curved and straight lines.

Paint and print

- *Paint tracks:* Place different-sized plastic vehicles with interesting tyre tracks in shallow trays of paint. Make them drive over the paper and leave paint tracks everywhere.
- *Train tracks:* Use strips of corrugated card to print train tracks all over the paper. Drive toy trains along the tracks.
- *Rollerball painting:* Provide empty glass deodorant bottles filled with different coloured runny paint. Roll the balls over paper to create patterns and pictures.
- *Sand tracks:* Use sit and ride vehicles to drive through sand, mud or water to create tracks in the playground.

Collage

- *Stop! Go! Give way!:* Observe road signs with the children. Look at the shapes used - triangles, rectangles, circles, etc. Use a range of shapes in red, black and white to design and create new road signs!

Modelling

- *Boxed in:* Provide a variety of different shaped boxes and talk about different vehicles. Could the box become a bus, a train or a car? Use a variety of shapes to fix onto the vehicle - circles for wheels, rectangles for a windscreen, doors, etc. Paint and embellish with metallic trims and foil, maybe even a number plate!
- *Wooden vehicles:* Help children to use thin balsa wood, bottle lids, nails and hammers to construct different vehicles. Can they make their vehicles move?

Clay and dough

- *Press and go:* Roll out a square tile of clay or dough and create a printed picture of a vehicle. Use cotton reels, bottle tops, etc. for wheels. Use stiff card edges to create lines or draw in windows and doors using clay tools. How could the children add headlights, a trailer, tyre treads, or drivers?

Famous Art

Piet Mondrian
– Broadway Boogie-Woogie

Get Set Go: Observe the simple shapes and primary colours in the painting. They are actually abstract roads and vehicles making journeys! Trace a journey around the picture. Use printing blocks, sponges, square-tipped brushes to create a new 'boogie-woogie'! Where will the road go? Which vehicles will be travelling?

Dance and Movement

Warm Up

 Go for a walk to an imaginary destination. How many different ways can you can move; giant steps, tip toes, backwards. Encourage the children's own suggestions.

Dance

Motor madness
Perform different types of transport. Start with slower forms such as walking, jogging, running and riding a bike. Build up to faster forms so actions become more intense and animated. Explore the different ways transport moves – on water with gliding movements, in the air flying, on rails keeping to tracks with rhythmical movements and on the roads stopping and starting.

Wheels on the bus
Perform this song whilst moving around the room as if on a bus travelling through the town or countryside. Encourage the children to form a line and follow a chosen driver. If there are lots of children then form several buses.

Variations;

The wheels on the train go super fast, the doors on the train slide open and shut

The wings on the plane go zoom zoom zoom; the hostess on the plane says "Any more drinks?"

The pedals on the bike spin round and round, the bell on the bike goes ding ding ding

Going on a journey
Children enjoy lining up rows of chairs two by two, and pretending to be in a vehicle. Invite the children to collect chairs and other suitable props to create a chosen vehicle. Give the children access to dressing up clothes. Start by setting the scene – let's wait at the bus stop. Let's climb on board and buy a ticket. Where shall we sit? Where are we going? Pretend to look out of the windows. Who is getting on and off the bus? A sound effects CD of a busy road, road works and sounds of the town and countryside will enhance the performance.

Movement games

Traffic Lights
One child is elected to be the Traffic Lights. The other children move around the room freely until the traffic lights call an instruction

RED – the children stop moving; AMBER – the children move very slowly; GREEN – the children move quickly; TRAFFIC JAM – all children line up holding onto the child in front of them. Change the traffic lights frequently to give other children an opportunity.

Cool Down

Some children will enjoy performing these individually standing up in front of the group. Alternatively sit quietly as a group to perform together.

Twinkle Twinkle traffic lights
(open and close hands as if flashing lights)
On the corner shining bright
Red means stop
(hold one hand out in a stop motion)
Green means go
(wave your hand as if showing traffic to move on)
Amber means go very slow
(sing this part slowly)

Twinkle Twinkle traffic lights
On the corner shining bright
(Sing to tune of Twinkle Twinkle)

Light

Drama and Role Play

Drama games

- *Pass the torch:* Sit in a circle and pass a torch around the circle as you sing this song to the tune of *Three Blind Mice*:
  Pass the torch X2
  Switch on the light X2
  Can you pull a silly face?
  Can you pull a funny face?
  Can you pull a scary face?
  Give me a fright!
  The child holding the torch at the end of the song can shine the light up under their chin and pull a face of their choice.

- *Warm up 1, 2, 3:* Try this warm up game. Ask children to stand in a circle and then walk round. Tap the tambourine once to change direction. When they are confident with this add a further instruction: tap the tambourine twice to change speed. Finally, tap three times to change the level at which they are traveling. This final stage is quite challenging for young children so don't introduce it until they are ready.

Mime

- *Blind pairs:* Talk to the children about what it must be like not to be able to see anything, including light. Ask them to work with a partner. Blindfold one of the children and ask their partner to lead them around the room taking care they don't trip or bump into anything or anybody.

Drama skills

- *Dark and light:* Choose different activities to try with eyes closed or wearing a blindfold and then repeat 'in the light' – putting on shoes, writing their name, having a drink, or walking across the room.

Role-play

A dark cave

Set up: Dark drapes, curtains and screens to create a 'cave' space, home corner furniture, cushions, luminous stars and shapes, lanterns, torches, lamps, soft-toy bears, bear masks or dressing-up suits.

Roles: Cave dwellers, bears, explorers.

Stories: A midnight snack in the cave by lamplight; explorers looking for treasure find a cave. A group of children are playing by the sea, the tide comes in and they hide in the cave. A family of bears hibernate in the cave waiting for spring to come. Act out the story of *Can't You Sleep, Little Bear* by Martin Waddell.

Stories, Songs and Rhymes

Stories

By The Light Of The Moon by Sheridan Cain
Act out the story helping Little Mouse to find a new nest.

Lights Out! Shadow Pop-Up And Play by Richard Fowler
Make shadow pictures using hands, objects and torches, or other light sources. Then make outlines from black sugar paper to shine a light through.

How To Catch A Star by Oliver Jeffers
Try painting pictures using the original, bold watercolour style in the book.

Lighting A Lamp by Jonny Zucker
Make diva lamps for Divali using painted clay and tea lights.

Songs and rhymes

- Starlight, Starbright
- Twinkle, Twinkle Little Star
- Up The Tall White Candlestick

Five Fizzing Fireworks

Five fizzing fireworks,
(Hold up five fingers)
Sparkling high
(Wiggle fingers)
In the dark November sky.
One went bang!
(Clap hands)
And shone so bright,
(Make a big circle with hands)
Lighting up the cold, dark night.

Four fizzing fireworks…

Switch My Torch On

(Tune: Wind The Bobbin Up)
Switch my torch on
Switch my torch on
In the middle of the night.
Shine it on the ceiling.
Shine it on the floor.
Shine it on my face.
And shine it on the door.
When the door opens,
I quickly go quiet,
Dive under the duvet
And switch off the light.

Three Bright Lights

(Tune: Three Blind Mice)
Three bright lights
Three bright lights
Sun, stars and moon,
Sun, stars and moon,
They all light up the sky so high
At different times of day
and night
Did you ever see such
a wonderful sight
As three bright lights?

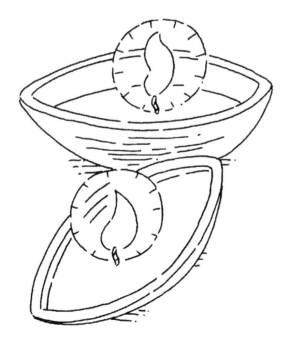

Design, Art and Modelling

Pencils and pens

- *Indian Diva lamps:* Make a simple template of a diva lamp (traditionally a small clay pot with a candle inside). Ask children to cut out a diva from card and stick onto paper using blutak. Push brightly coloured chalks outwards from the template and smudge and blend to create rays of light. Remove the template.

Paint and print

- *Painted lampshades:* Buy cheap paper, fabric or plastic lampshades and paint designs onto them. Mix pva glue with paint to create a longer lasting effect.
- *Tints of light:* Add light to a favourite colour. Start with the base colour at its darkest and paint a stripe. Add increasing amounts of white, painting a stripe each time. Watch as the colour gets lighter.

Collage

- *Stained glass windows:* Make simple stained glass windows using coloured tissue, films and plastics. Use black paper to cut out a traditional church window frame. Cut and shape the coloured materials and stick them over the holes. Hang up in the window and watch the light change colour.

Modelling

- *Sparkle sticks:* Fix a range of gold, orange, yellow and silver ribbons, tinsel and strips of wrapping paper into the end of a cardboard tube. Shake it in the light and watch it twinkle. Make up a firework dance and use your sparkle sticks!
- *Divali mirrors:* Help children to fold a square of thin card and cut out semi circles along the crease. Re-fold the card and repeat the cuts. Re-fold the card diagonally and repeat the cuts and fold diagonally again. Unfold to find a star of circles. Mount onto a piece of silver foil and embellish with sequins.

Clay and dough

- *Pasta candlesticks:* Make simple clay candlesticks. Make the base by flattening one side of a small fist-sized ball of clay so it can stand steady. Push the candle into the top to make a hole. Decorate the base with pieces of dried pasta. Spray with gold or silver paint or paint and varnish with watered-down pva glue.

Famous Art

Giacomo Balla - Street Light

Camera artwork: Take a photograph of a burning candle. Use light coloured pastels and chalks on dark paper to try and recreate a picture of a candle or streetlight.

Dance and Movement

Warm Up

Let's act out being the sun rising up in the morning, stretching out wide and shining using fingers wiggling, maybe disappearing behind a cloud, the rain comes and a beautiful rainbow appears, before setting again in the evening creeping down below the horizon. Encourage the children to make up their own movements and stories for the sun.

Dance

Spooky torches

In a darkened room give the children hand torches to dance about with. Halloween type music can provide added atmosphere for this activity.

Five flickering candles
(Sing to the tune of 10 green bottles)

Five flickering candles standing in a row x 2
But if the wind should accidently blow......... SMASH!
There'd be four flickering candles standing in a row
Continue with three flickering candles and so on…
Invite the children to be the candles flickering in the wind and then falling from the wall and smashing to the ground.

Movement Games

Lighthouse keeper

Create dens by placing sheets over tables around the room ensuring all other obstacles are removed before starting. One child is chosen to be the Lighthouse Keeper and they are given a torch. The lighthouse keeper calls out actions for the other children to perform such as dancing, wiggling, jumping hopping and so on. At any point the lighthouse keeper can switch on the torch and shout out "STORM COMING" where upon all children must run and hide in a den.

Cool Down

In a darkened room shine a light onto the wall and show children how they can create shadows using their hands and fingers. A simple butterfly is a good starting point. More confident children may like to try making their shadows dance.

Machines

Drama games

- Sit in a circle and pass machine sounds around the ring. Use machine voices to greet each other and ask questions.
- *Pass the phone:* Pass a mobile phone around the circle until it rings. Ask for a volunteer to make the ringtone. The child who pretends to answer it must improvise a conversation or argument.
- *Phone moods:* As before pass a phone around the circle. Invite children to pretend that they are hearing bad, happy, sad or worrying news. How will they respond?

Mime

- *Remote control:* Ask children to find a space in the room. Explain that you have the remote control and that they are machines and have to do what you say, immediately! Give one-word instructions such as: walk, forwards, backwards, jump, hop, up, down, stand, sit, spin. Invite confident children to have a turn at being in control of the machines.

- *What's my machine?:* Invite children to mime using a machine for the others to guess. Try miming using a mobile phone, camera, computer, calculator, kettle, toaster, mixer, hairdryer, hoover, drill, mower, and so on.

Drama skills

- Ask each child to create a machine sound, and then add a repeated movement like a machine. Ask them to work with a partner and combine their sounds and movements together. Go round and switch the machines on and off.
- *Group machines:* Join the children together to form a group machine. Make the movements interact and synchronized. Give each child a number and ask them to start making their sound and movement when they hear their number. Use the numbers to start and stop the group machine.

Role-play

Factory floor

Set up: Make a giant machine using a climbing frame, slide, A-frame, ladders, hoops, balance beam etc. Add a conveyor belt and buttons to press.

Roles: Foreman, workers, objects going through the machine.

Stories: The workers go on strike; the machine changes speed, either very fast or slow, and then breaks down; vary the finished product that each machine makes from cars or toys to baked beans; somebody gets hurt in the machine.

Stories

Duck in the Truck by Jez Alborough
Act out the story.

Amazing Machines by Tony Mitton
Use words from the book to create sound effects using vocal and body percussion or instruments.

Mole Machines by Judith Harries
Design and construct machines from a variety of materials.

Mole Machines

Farmer Huntley needed help. His tractor had broken down. "I need a new machine to dig up the potatoes" he said. "I shall give a reward to anyone who can invent a machine to help me." So he put up a poster advertising the competition all over the farm.

Carla Cow decided to have a go. She fixed together two wheels and a length of piping to make a machine, but it got stuck in the mud and a wheel fell off.

Harry Horse thought he could do better. He fixed together four wheels, a coat hanger and a spade to make a machine, but the spade snapped in half.

Felix Fox was very clever. He fixed together a ladder, a shovel and a battery to make a machine, but the rungs of the ladder were rotten and broke.

Monty Mole smiled to himself. He had a really good idea for a digging machine. And so, he sharpened his claws, polished his nose, and began to dig. Farmer Huntley and the other animals were all very impressed with Monty and decided that the best digging machine of all had in fact been right under their noses!

Songs and rhymes

- Down By The Station
- The Wheels On The Bus
- Hickory Dickory Dock

Robot, Robot Turn Around

(Tune: We Three Kings)
See my robot marching around
See my robot making a sound
Wheels-a-turning, cogs-a-whirring
Spinning on the ground.
Oh robot, robot turn around.
Robot, robot make a sound.
Left and right and up and down.
Robot, robot turn around.

The Wheels On My Machine

(Tune: The Wheels On The Bus)
The wheels on my machine go round and round
Round and round, round and round.
The wheels on my machine go round and round,
All day long.

The lights on my machine flash on and off…
The buttons on my machine switch up and down…

Pencils and pens

- *Working diagrams:* Help children to take apart some small machines such as clocks, old telephones, radios. Ask them to draw diagrams of what they can see inside.
- *Springing:* Look at different-sized springs. Try pulling and stretching them. Draw lots of spiralling springs using metallic pens and crayons on black paper.

Paint and print

- *Paint spinning:* Put a paper plate inside a salad spinner. Drop different coloured blobs of thin paint onto the plate, put the lid on the spinner, turn the handle and watch the paint fly around. Remove and display the paper plate art.
- *Press prints:* Use a blunt pencil or old biro to draw a simple picture or design of a machine, cog, wheel, etc. onto a polystyrene tile. Use black printing ink and rollers and print onto white paper. Add silver paint to the finished print.

Collage

- *Moving machines:* Provide corrugated cardboard, string, cardboard cogs and wheels, cotton reels, buttons and split pins to design moving machine collages. Which parts of the machine moves?
- *Staple art:* Work in a group to cut up strips and shapes of paper, card and felt and staple together in different ways.

Modelling

- *Junk machines:* Use different sized boxes, cardboard tubes, buttons, straws, plastic and metal bottle tops, glue, paint and scissors, etc. Create small machines such as mobile phones, walky talkies, clocks, calculators, radios, etc. to use in role play activities.
- *Giant robot:* As a group use large cardboard boxes, buttons, aluminium foil, egg boxes, plastic trays from cakes and biscuits to construct a giant robot. Paint with silver and gold paint.

Clay and dough

- *Iron man:* Build a robot shape from clay and add metal nuts and bolts, screws, paper clips, garden wire, split pins, springs, washers, buttons, pipe cleaners.

Famous Art

Robots - film by Twentieth Century Fox
My plastic robot: Make a mini-robot using plastic bottles, yoghurt pots, tubes, plastic lids, bendy drinking straws, scrunchy trays.

Dance and Movement

Warm Up

 Sitting in pairs get the children performing pulling and pushing actions. Extend this to form a group circle and repeat actions. Create movements together that remind the children of machines – hammering, spinning, pulling, cutting, and crushing and so on.

Dance

Dance along to Bob the Builder's "Can we fix it?" creating actions to match the lyrics.

A twist on the traditional "If You're Happy and You Know It", create your own version with actions to match machines familiar to the children. For example;

If you're happy and you know it do the hoovering (motion using the vacuum cleaner), do the washing (spin arms like the washing spinning round and round), dry your hair (motion using a hair dryer). How many more actions and machines can the children come up with?

Movement games

Washing Machine
You will need a parachute. Half the children are the washing and the other half are the machine. The machine children stand holding the parachute. In goes the washing (washing children sit under the parachute) in goes the powder and mix (give the parachute a really good shake about). Start the washing cycle (children holding the parachute run round in a circle first one way then the other way. Rinse the clothes (shake) and then dry (move the parachute up and down with big movements). Repeat the actions with children reversing their roles.

Cool Down

Pretend you are a machine. Discuss as a group how machines might move. Allow the children to move about in any way they wish providing movements are slow and controlled to ensure children have time to stretch and calm down. You could suggest big heavy machines such as a big steam roller, or a ploughing tractor to further promote slower movements.

Materials

Drama games

- Display a collection of different items made from a variety of materials. Ask one child to choose one item, place it into a bag without being seen by the others, and then describe it to the rest of the group by touch. Can they guess what is in the bag? See the topic of Senses.
- *Sticky feet:* Improve children's posture and deportment using this fun game. Pretend to apply super glue to the children's feet so that they are stuck firm to the floor. Stick them in different positions, close together, far apart, hip width apart: which is the most stable?

Mime

- *Sculptors:* Ask children to work with a partner, one is the sculptor, one the clay. Invite them to sculpt the clay into sculptures using different materials, wood, clay, metal, junk, sand etc. Once the sculpture is ready can the others guess what it is?

Drama skills

- *Waxwork museum:* Describe to the children a museum or collection of statues and then ask them to model themselves into a statue or use some statues from the Sculptors game above. Start with various characters from stories or different sports. Walk round and see if you can identify what the children have become. On a signal ask the statues to come alive, and act or mime their character or sport to help them be identified.
- Improvise a drama about the museum where one day or night the waxworks all come to life by magic and scare the visitors or the curator.

Role-play

A builder's yard or building site

Set up: Bricks, wood, sand, gravel, buckets, tools, spades, pipes, rulers, measures, striped tape, string, ladders, cones, wheelbarrow, signs, spirit levels, paint brushes, tins of paint, overalls, hard hats, boots, plans, stripey workman's hut, wall paper, paint charts, tea-making equipment etc. Home-made bricks made from small cardboard boxes stuffed with newspaper that are sealed and wrapped in brown paper.

Roles: Manager, foreman, architect, builders, workmen, customers.

Stories: Somebody gets injured on the site when tools are left lying around, work is delayed. Poor quality materials and a wall falls down. There is a mistake in the plans and the door is in the wrong place. Celebrate the opening of the new building. Act out some *Bob the Builder* stories

Stories

The Three Little Pigs Traditional
Make collage houses using different materials such as art straws; lolipop sticks and twigs; and printed Duplo bricks.

Stone Soup Traditional
Act out the story.

The Wooden Dragon by Joan Aiken
Use clay and other modeling material to create baby dragons.

Painted Pebbles by Judith Harries
Try painting some pebbles.

Painted Pebbles

Adam loved painting. He painted all the time. At nursery he painted pictures at the easel. At home he painted pictures at the kitchen table. Mummy put them on the fridge or took them to work to brighten up her office. In the bathroom he painted on the tiles with special bath paints. In the garden he painted with water on the wall. In the holidays, at grandma's house, Adam painted her wooden chair. "Oh dear Adam! That was my favourite chair!" They scrubbed it with soapy water but the paint would not come off. Grandma sighed and then said "I have an idea; let's go down to the beach and find something to paint." Adam was confused. He couldn't think of anything he could paint at the beach.

Grandma walked along the shingle, away from her usual spot on the sand, and bent down to pick up stones. "That's a good one" she

said, as she dropped a pebble into Adam's plastic bucket. Adam followed her up and down the beach but couldn't guess what she was planning.

Back in grandma's kitchen, she showed him how to paint the pebbles and turn them into different creatures. Adam painted with a big smile on his face. He knew that he would never run out of pebbles to paint.

Songs and rhymes

- Peter Hammers With One Hammer
- There's A Hole In My Bucket
- London Bridge Is Falling Down
- Humpty Dumpty

Materials

(Tune: My Hat It Has Three Corners)
My hat is made of felt,
My scarf is made of wool,
My gloves are made of leather,
And they all keep me warm.
My house is made of bricks,
My roof is made of tiles,
My windows are made of glass,
And they all make my home.

The triangle is made of metal
The claves are made of wood
The castanets are made of plastic
And they all make good sounds.

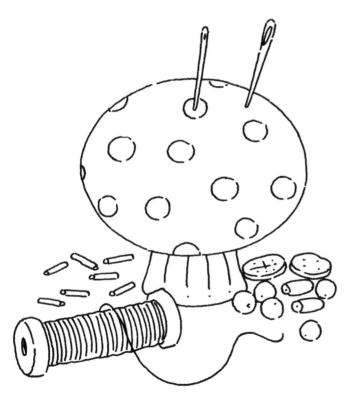

Design, Art and Modelling

Pencils and pens

- *Mexican metal work:* Help children to cut the base off a foil dish and tape the sharp edges. Place the foil tile onto a magazine or mouse mat. Use clay tools, pencils, or the tip of a paintbrush to press marks and patterns into the foil. Feel the pattern on the underside! Add colour using permanent markers.

Paint and print

- *Materials:* Paint and print with different materials such as bubble wrap, felt, rags, sponges, netting, lace and fabric. Knot and twist the materials to make dabbers to dip into paint. Swirl, splodge and drag across the paper. How many different effects can the children create?
- *Finger fun:* Make finger paint from powder paint mixed with water, flour and a small amount of liquid soap. Spread the mixture onto a tray and have fun finger painting. Blob it, print it, make patterns and swirls. Don't forget to have paper handy in case children want to make some more permanent marks.

Collage

- *Sewing sampler:* Stretch old leg of tights over a small wire ring or embroidery frame. Pull it taut and then show children how to use a large blunt needle threaded with wool to sew. Make big loopy stitches using lots of different colours.
- *Binka bar mats:* Provide coaster sized pieces of binka (customised fabric for beginner sewers) and try some simple cross stitch patterns using different coloured embroidery threads.

Modelling

- *African starch resist:* Use good quality calico or old cotton sheets cut into squares using pinking shears. Make a mixture of flour and water (runny consistency) and fill empty washing up liquid bottles with the mixture. Squirt simple patterns. Leave to dry completely (near to a radiator or outside in the sun) until the starch begins to crack. Paint over the patterns and leave to dry once more. Peel and rub off the starch mix and watch the patterns appear underneath.

Clay and dough

- *D.I.Y. playdough:* Use this recipe to make some playdough with the children: 1 cup of flour, 1 cup of water, 2 teaspoons of cream of tartar, 1 teaspoon of oil, food colouring. Mix ingredients together over a low heat until the dough blends. Knead until smooth and leave to cool.

Famous Art

Jeannie Baker – Window (picture book with collage illustrations)

Material mayhem: Use the images from the book as a starting pointfor material work. Use a collection of materials to make tactile pictures. Add a window frame.

Dance and Movement

Warm Up

The object of the warm up is to move about in the style of different materials, for example wood, rubber, metal (robotic), light floating fabrics such as chiffon or stretchy fabric such as Lycra. How many different types of materials and movements can the children create?

Dance

Discovering fabrics
Supply the children with a wide range of different materials to act as props to their dance. Play differing tempos of music to encourage the children to move about with the materials. Tranquil music may suit light floating fabrics encouraging swaying, leisurely movements, whilst upbeat fast music may suit Lycra encouraging stretching and bouncing, and a brisk and lively dance.

Movement Games

Parachute play
As the children hold the parachute encourage them to move it up and down. Once they are confident with this movement add small plastic balls onto the top of the parachute and see how quickly the balls can be shaken off. Repeat this action with different objects of differing materials

e.g. balloons or shredded paper.Any game involving the parachute will enhance children's understanding of how fabrics move. Invite children to suggest ways to move the parachute about.

Cool Down

Imagine you are a sculpture made of ice remaining very still and frozen. Explain to the children that the sun is shining brightly and all the ice sculptures are going to slowly melt into a puddle of water.

Minibeasts

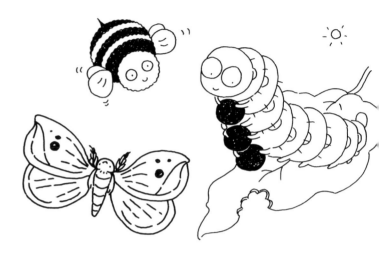

Drama games

- *Life cycles:* Talk about the different stages of growth involved in a lifecycle of a frog or butterfly. Introduce terms such as egg, caterpillar, pupa, butterfly. Sit in a circle and ask children to say the words in the correct order around the ring. Add actions. Anyone who gets it wrong has to sit out.

Mime

- *Minibeast Moves:* A fast-moving miming game in the style of 'Beans'. Call out names of different minibeasts for children to mime. Start with a butterfly – flying around the room, a bee – buzzing as they fly, a worm – wiggling on the ground, a caterpillar – crawling on all fours. When the children are confident with these add more such as a ladybird – walking daintily on tip-toe, a flea or frog – jumping, a snail – sliding around the floor, a spider – join with a partner on all fours to create eight legs, and finally a centipede – all join together in a long line with hands around waists.

Drama skills

- *Little Miss Muffet:* Act out the nursery rhyme and help children to show different emotions. Start quite happy when Miss Muffet is eating her supper and then change to 'fear' when the spider arrives. Can the children think of a way of changing the rhyme in order to change the moods?
- Improvise a drama when the children are magically reduced in size and find themselves in a garden where they encounter lots of different minibeasts? What would they see, hear, feel, etc? How could they get back to their original size and world?

Role-play

Minibeasts' garden or jungle

Set up: Trees and plants made from corrugated cardboard, and green crepe paper, hanging creepers, butterfly nets, holes in tree trunks, green or brown mats, soft-toy birds and plastic bugs. Make an entrance way through a curtain made of green streamers or garden netting. Make home-made bugs made from cardboard circles, pipe-cleaners, net wings, buttons, etc.

Roles: Explorers, visitors, minibeasts.

Stories: Discover a brand new minibeast in the jungle; get bitten or stung by a bug; imagine life as a tiny minibeast, escaping from predators and humans!

Stories

The Very Hungry Caterpillar by Eric Carle
Look at the changes in the book from an egg to a caterpillar, a pupa to a butterfly and make a lifecycle wheel.

The Bad-Tempered Ladybird by Eric Carle
Talk about and act out the change in the ladybird as it meets the different animals in the story.

Anansi The Spider Traditional Caribbean
Make model spiders from egg-boxes and pipe cleaners.

Tadpole's Promise by Jeanne Willis
Use brightly coloured felt or sweet-wrappers to create collages of rainbow caterpillars.

Songs and rhymes

- There's A Worm At The Bottom Of My Garden
- Little Arabella Miller
- Incy Wincy Spider
- Little Miss Muffet
- There Was An Old Woman Who Swallowed A Fly

What A Lot Of Bugs

(Finger rhyme)

Buzzing bees, flying flies,
Darting dragonflies.
Wiggling worms, spinning spiders,
Crawling caterpillars.
Slow snails, lazy ladybirds,
Silly centipedes.
Bustling beetles, slithering slugs,
What a lot of bugs!

A Very Hungry Caterpillar

(Tune: original)

A very hungry caterpillar sat upon a leaf,
Munch, munch, munch, munch, munch, munch, munch.
A very hungry caterpillar sat upon a leaf,
Munch, munch, munch, munch eating his lunch.

The caterpillar got much fatter and he span around.
Spin, spin, spin, spin, spin, spin, spin.
The caterpillar got much fatter and he span around.
Spin, spin, spin, spin. Like a pin.

A dry and brown pupa case fell upon the ground.
There it lay without a sound.

A dry and brown pupa case fell upon the ground.
There it lay without a sound.

A rainbow-coloured butterfly flew into the air.
Flap, flap, flap, flap, flap, flap, flap.
A rainbow-coloured butterfly flew into the air.
Flap, flap, flap, flap, flap, flap, flap.

Design, Art and Modelling

Pencils and pens

- *Chalk butterflies:* Using small pieces of chalk, place them lengthwise on a piece of paper and press and twist to create a simple butterfly shape with two wings. Draw in a body and antennae using black felt pen. Repeat with different colours and sizes of chalk.

Paint and print

- *Butterfly paintings:* Ask children to fold paper in half and then open it out. Paint blobs and lines on one side of the paper and then fold the paper over and press. Cut out the wing shapes of the butterfly and admire the symmetry!

Collage

- *Glitter webs:* Put runny pva glue into a squeezy bottle and drizzle around the inside of a round plastic lid.

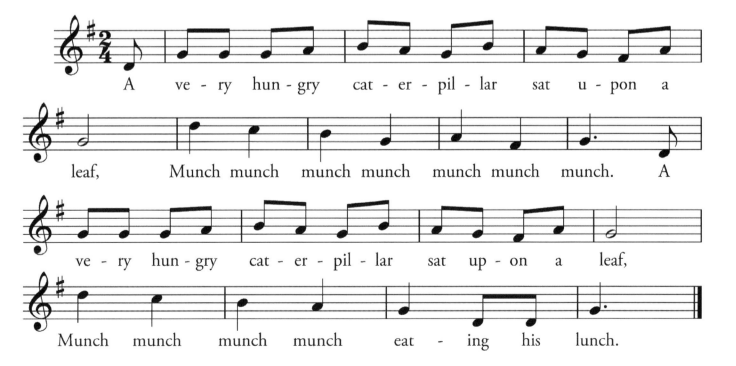

Make several concentric circles and then four lines cutting across to create the shape of a spider web. Sprinkle glitter onto the glue and leave to dry. Carefully peel off the web and hang on windows.

Modelling

- *Egg box bugs:* Use strips of egg boxes to create caterpillars or centipedes. Paint each segment in a different colour and add pipe cleaner legs. Paint single egg boxes red with black spots and make ladybirds, or black and use four pipe cleaners for a spider's eight legs. Hang on giant webs made from plastic hoops strung with wool or string.
- *Concertina caterpillars:* Cut two long strips of paper in two contrasting colours. Staple them together into an L shape and then fold over each one alternately to create a long spring.

Clay and dough

- *Dough bugs:* Use clay or dough to make different bugs. Take a small ball of dough and add matchsticks for legs and buttons for eyes. Add spots and patterns using clay tools.

Famous Art

www.dkimages.com
- photographs of insects

Minibeast portraits: Choose a favourite photograph of an insect and paint a giant portrait using household brushes and bright coloured paints.

Dance and Movement

Warm Up

Pretend you are caterpillars in chrysalises curled up small. Slowly emerge and spread out your wings. Gently flutter around exploring the environment.

Dance

Ugly Bug Ball
You will need a copy of this popular piece of music. Each child chooses an insect they wish to be, remembering the insects in the song. Discuss with the children how their individual insects move about. They may choose to be a fluttering butterfly, a spinning spider or a hopping cricket.

Play the music allowing the children to dance freely, interpreting the music in their own way. Older children or children very familiar with the song may act out the story told within the music. Appropriate dressing up clothes or light floating fabrics can enhance the children's imagination of their chosen minibeast.

Flight of the Bumble Bee
Play the classical piece "Flight of the Bumble Bee" by Rimsky–Korsakov. Invite the children to dance and move around the room like busy bees. Encourage them to act out flying, scurrying, crawling, buzzing, landing on flowers to collect nectar, returning to their hive and so on.

Movement Games

Ladybird Leaves
Using a variety of coloured and textured construction paper invite the children to create large leaves. Spread the leaves out evenly upon the floor. The children move around as ladybirds whilst lively music is played. When the music stops they must fly quickly to a leaf. Removing a leaf each time means children will gather in groups on a single leaf. Alternatively – as with musical chairs, each time the music stops remove a leaf. The child left without a leaf is "out".

Creepy Crawlies
Create a starting line and a finishing line. The children race in the style of a mini beast. For example wiggling worms on their bellies, scuttling beetles crouched down low with tiny steps or web building spiders spinning round. Alternatively create a course to move through. Outdoors this is simply done with marking out a course on the ground in chalk.

Spider webs
Invite the children to form a circle standing up. One child starts with a ball of wool. Keeping hold of the end of the string of wool in one hand they throw the ball to another child in the circle. This child in turn holds their piece of wool and throws the ball to yet another child. Keep repeating this action to include all children. As the ball of wool moves from one child to another it creates a spider's web effect in the middle of the circle.

Cool Down

Using a rope or chalk mark out a giant spider web. A simple spiral shape works well. The children walk/balance along the web until they reach the middle. Encourage the children to create their own webs to conquer. Find different ways of moving along the web.

Night

Drama games

- *Chinese night whispers:* Sit in a circle and pass a nighttime message around the circle very quietly. Does it stay the same?
- *Drama in the dark:* Make the room as dark as possible and let the children get used to it. Ask them to stand in a space. Play peaceful music to set the scene for 'night'. Invite the children to move slowly around the room, taking care not to bump into anybody. Help any nervous children by holding their hand or letting them go round with a friend. Ask them to pretend to be nocturnal creatures such as foxes, cats and badgers creeping about, or bats and owls flying around. End the game by curling up on the floor and having a quick sleep!

Mime

- *What's my line at night?:* Invite children to mime doing different jobs that happen during the night such as nurses, doctors, milkmen, postmen, lorry drivers and police officers.
- *Throw that feeling:* See the topic of Friends.

Drama skills

- *Night characters:* Ask children to work with a partner, each with a prop, and improvise a bedtime adventure. Suitable props could be a torch, umbrella, toothbrush, story book, teddy bear, toy, mug, candle, pillow, telescope etc.
- Improvise a night drama. Choose some characters to go on a night walk, hear some strange sounds, become very scared. What do the noises turn out to be?

Role-play

Home corner at night

Set up: Home corner furniture, black-out curtains or windows, pyjamas, dressing-gowns, slippers, cocoa, biscuits, a television, bed, duvets, pillows, lamps, torch, toothbrushes, storybooks, clock.

Roles: Family members, children, babysitter, visitors etc.

Stories: Different bedtime situations: somebody doesn't want to go to bed; someone refuses to brush their teeth or insists on another story; a child plays up to the babysitter. Create a peaceful bedtime scene with a child cuddled up for a cosy story when they hear a strange noise downstairs, is it a burglar? Act out the story of *Peace At Last* by Jill Murphy.

Stories

 Night Monkey, Day Monkey by Julia Donaldson
Paint contrasting pictures of night and day.

 Can't You Sleep, Little Bear? by Martin Waddell
Act out the story as Little Bear struggles to sleep and Big Bear helps him not to be afraid of the dark.

 Peace At Last by Jill Murphy
Use musical instruments to create sound effects for all the sounds of the night that keep Mr. Bear awake.

The Baby Who Wouldn't Go To Bed
by Helen Cooper
Act out the story of the baby driving
around in his red car to avoid going to bed!

Songs
and rhymes

- Diddle Diddle Dumpling
- Twinkle Twinkle Little Star
- Golden Slumbers

One Dark Dark Night

(Tune: original)
One dark dark night
When the stars were shining bright
I heard a sound
I saw a sight
One dark dark night.

One dark dark night
When the stars were shining bright
I felt a touch
I had a fright
One dark dark night.

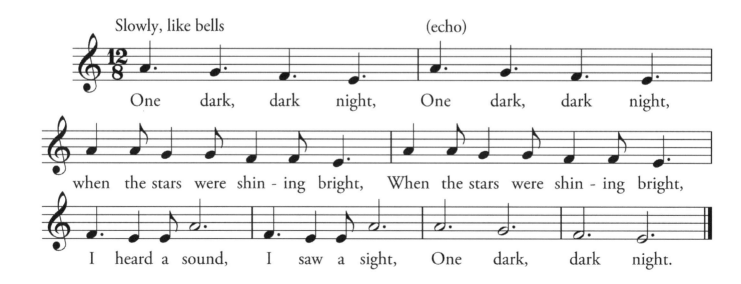

Stepping Stones to Creativity

Pencils and pens

- *Street lights:* Ask children to draw a night time street scene. Include car headlamps, traffic lights, shop fronts and street lamps. Use black paper and a range of metallic crayons and chalks in reds, oranges and whites.

Paint and print

- *The sky at night:* Encourage children to observe the night sky at bedtime and talk about their observations. Use a range of dark papers and paint to create a night sky. Blow orange, white, yellow and gold paint through straws, or splatter using brushes to depict the sky at night.

Collage

- *Night owls:* Use oval and circle templates to make an owls body, head and wings. Select real and handmade feathers in brown, white and black. Make feathers by fringing strips of thin paper. Arrange and glue all the feathers into place. Add big yellow or amber eyes and a sharp beak made from a folded diamond piece of card to complete your night owl.
- *Moon and stars:* Cut full or crescent moon and star shapes from thin card using templates (see templates at the back of this book). Stick a range of shiny papers, cellophane, wrapping paper and holographic materials onto them. Make a small hole through the top and suspend from either a hoop or stick.

Modelling

- *Night scene:* Use a small cereal or shoe box and cut out the front leaving a thin frame all round. Paint the inside of the box in black and dark blues and leave to dry. Use sequins, beads, sticky stars, metallic pens, etc to decorate the inside like the night sky. Suspend different shapes in the foreground from a string at the top such as a bird, owl, bat, plane, moon, or even a ghost.

Clay and dough

- *Night lights:* Make a small ball of clay and push a hole into it using a small tea light. Decorate the clay with patterns using tools, matchsticks, forks, etc. Leave to air dry or fire. Spray or paint the dry pot with luminous paint. These lights should really glow in the dark!

Famous Art

Vincent Van Gogh – The Starry Night

Night night: Observe the painting and discuss how the street and its' buildings seem darker at night. Ask children to paint their own house or street at night. Use a darker palette of colours and experiment by adding black and navy blue to give a dark, night time feel to the painting.

Warm Up

 Imagine you are getting ready for bed. Exaggerate each movement as you get changed into your pyjamas, dressing gown and slippers. Maybe you need to wash your face and brush your teeth. Play quiet lullaby music as the children perform.

Dance

 Disco Beat
Bop and groove to the classic disco tune "Night Fever"

Brahm's Lullaby (Waltz No 15)
Encourage children to dance quietly to this lullaby music. Some suggestions include: up on tip toes, fingers on lips, baby steps, crouched down low and slowly creeping

Movement games

Musical Pillows
Play as you would musical chairs, simply replacing the chairs with pillows. Children could bring in a pillow from home.

Bouncing on the bed
Play as you would musical bumps but imagine you are bouncing on a big bed whilst the music plays

Cool Down

 Choose some quiet lullaby music and darken the room to give a feeling of bedtime. Invite children to dance quietly about the room. Maybe they could pretend to be twinkling stars in the night sky or fireflies fluttering about and shining the way brightly.

Numbers

Drama and Role Play

Drama games

- *Buzz 1 2 3:* Stand in a circle and count '1', '2', '3', 'buzz' round the ring. Those who say 'buzz' have to sit down. Who is left standing at the end?
- *Huggy 2, 3, 4:* This is a great warm-up game for breaking the ice! Ask children to move around the room taking care not to touch anybody else until they hear you shout out 'Huggy 2'. This is the signal to find a friend to hug. When they hear the shout 'Huggy 3' or 'Huggy 4' they have to get into a group of three or four and have a group hug!
- *Musical numbers:* Move to the music and when it stops find a partner and make the shape of a number in the air or on the floor. Decide on which number to make before the music begins again.

Mime

- *Moving numbers:* Give each child a number from 1 to 4. Ask all the number 4s to move across the room as though they are carrying something very heavy. Then ask all the number 1s to skip across the room. Ask all the 2s and 3s to make wheelbarrows and move together across the room. Think of different ways for each set of numbers to move.

Drama skills

- *Maps:* Help children to draw maps of islands on squared paper and add interesting places to visit. Number the squares along the top and side and select co-ordinates to choose a route around the island. Ask children to create a drama as they explore their maps.

Role-play

A row of terraced houses

Set up: Multiple sets of home corner furniture to create a row of houses, with separate front doors and different house numbers. Add sets of matching coloured props for each house and letters with the house numbers on. A postman hat and bag, sit-and-ride toys, boxes to deliver to houses.

Roles: Families, neighbours, a postman, delivery driver, visitors.

Stories: Families visiting their next-door neighbour; a letter or box delivered to the wrong address; a noisy party in one house, upsetting the neighbours.

Stories, Songs and Rhymes

Stories

Handa's Surprise by Eileen Browne
Create a series of paintings and collages to show the fruit bowl as the fruit gradually disappears.

Snow White and the seven dwarfs Traditional
Paint portraits of different dwarves, then label each one, frame and display.

Three Billy Goat's Gruff Traditional
Use three different sized toy goats to act out and retell the story. Ask children to design a really scary troll mask and then use in their drama.

One Hundred Hungry Ants by Elinor Pinczes
Use pen and ink to create numbers made from ants.

Songs and rhymes

- Five Fat Sausages
- Five Fat Peas In A Peapod Pressed
- Five Currant Buns
- 12345, Once I Caught A Fish Alive
- When I Was One I Ate A Bun
- Five Little Ducks
- Ten Green Bottles
- Going to St. Ives
- Hickory Dickory Dock

I Am Five Years Old Today

I am five years old today.
I am no longer four.
I'm feeling very grown up
And I can tell you more.
That now I'm five,
There's just one thing
I really want for me.
To be six years old,
And that's not all,
As quickly as can be!

Five Bright Candles

Five bright candles on a birthday cake.
1, 2, 345, there's really no mistake.
Take a big breath and away we go!
Out go the candles as we blow!

I Like To Count

(Tune: Bingo)
I like to count, there is no doubt
And counting is my game-o
1, 2, 345, 1, 2, 345, 1, 2, 345,
And counting is my game-o.

I like to count, there is no doubt
And counting is my game-o
6, 7, 8 9 10, 6, 7, 8 9 10, 6, 7, 8 9 10
And counting is my game-o.

I like to count, there is no doubt
I like counting backwards
10, 9, 876, 5,4,321, now there are no more
And counting is my game-o.

Design, Art and Modelling

Pencils and pens

- *Computer numbers:* Try some ICT art with the children. Using a computer keyboard, type in lots of different numbers into Word. Change fonts, colours and sizes to create a number display.

Paint and print

- *Painting by numbers:* Draw a simple outline picture and divide it into sections. Add numbers to each section. Help children to make up a key to show which colours correspond with each number and then they can ask a friend to colour or paint in the shapes.
- *Printing lists:* Ask children to follow instructions on a list and print different numbers of items as written. Try 3 corks, 4 bricks, 2 lids and 4 sponges. Ask them to write new lists for others to follow.

Collage

- *Dominoes:* Make a game of dominoes using cardboard, paint and other materials. Use small rectangles of card, draw a line across the centre and then paint or stick a number of dots on each half.

Modelling

- *Pasta jewellery:* Toss penne or straight macaroni pasta shapes in a small amount of food colouring until covered, and then leave to dry spread out on a tray for about an hour. Thread onto strong string or elastic and make repeated patterns such as 2 blue, 2 red, etc. or red, green, blue, etc.
- *Giant dice:* Paint a large square cardboard box a different colour on each face to make a giant cube. Then add dots

arranged in the traditional layout for a dice onto each face. Play a game using the dice.

Clay and dough

● *Happy birthday:* Make a cake shape from playdough and use small birthday candles to stick into the birthday cake. Sing happy birthday to a child or adult in the group.

Famous Art

Salvador Dali - Clock Explosion

Clockworks: Cut different-sized circles of card and create clock faces. Draw on hands and numbers using lots of colours and sizes. Stick together into in a giant confusion of clocks and numbers.

Dance and Movement

Warm Up

Say the name of each child. As you say it clap the syllables. Repeat by standing up and stamping out the names with your feet. Who has the shortest and the longest name? Notice the rhythms changing.

Dance

Ten in the bed

Invite children to lie in rows of ten on the floor. One by one the children roll away at the end of each verse. Use props - ten pillows or ten blankets and ask the children to count the objects before you sing. Singing along to a CD is always good fun and helps children to match movements to music.

Five little speckled frogs

Tape five lily pads cut from construction paper, to steps or a bench. Stand one child on each lily pad. Sing 5 little speckled frogs. At the end of each verse one child hops like a frog from his/her lily pad.

If you have lots of children have another set of 5 lily pads on another imaginary pond. Its nice to sing along to a CD as this can help the performance become more animated and the frogs can dance about too! Encourage the children to think about how frogs move with hopping and jumping actions.

Two by Two

You will need some traditional country dancing music. Stand the children in two lines so that each child is facing a partner. Make up simple dance sequences involving the

partners copying each other in time to the music. For example, clap hands twice, clap hands with your partner twice, bend your knees twice. Take two steps backwards then two steps forwards. What ever sequence you create continue to repeat the actions till the end of the music helping the children build confidence in what they are doing.

Movement Games

Number splats

For this game you will need ten pieces of card (preferably different colours) each labelled with a number from 1 to 10. The cards are stuck to the wall around the room – at the children's eye level! Gather the children in the middle of the room. Play a lively piece of music and invite the children to dance along. When the music is stopped call out a number from 1 to 10. The children must run to the appropriate number card.

Having different colours will help children less confident with number recognition to participate as you can also call out the colour card that is appropriate. Simply repeat this action until the music finishes or the last child to reach the called number can be "out". Encourage the children to move and dance about in different ways, perhaps suggesting to skip to the next number or to walk backwards.

Cool Down

Lying on the floor call out a number and an action, remembering to keep the actions slow and controlled. Suggested actions include a deep breath in and out, a lift of the arms or a bend of the knees. Invite the children to suggest cool down actions for everyone to perform.

Opposites

Drama games

- *Opposites word game:* Two children challenge each other to be the quickest to say the opposite to any word you say. The winner then has to be challenged by a new child.
- *No and Yes!:* This is challenging for young children. Ask a question that requires a yes or no answer and they must say the opposite answer, for instance 'are you a boy?' or 'have you got three legs?' Try not to laugh and that makes it even harder!

Mime

- *Mirror opposites:* See the topics of Food and Ourselves. Ask children to work with a partner. Whatever the partner mimes the mirror has to do the opposite! So if one lifts up their right hand and waves, the mirror does the same, but with the left hand etc.
- *Happy and sad masks:* Make some opposite mood masks such as happy/sad, angry/calm, scared/brave. Let the children wear the masks and mime a character to fit the mask.

Drama skills

- Ask children to work with a partner and make up a drama about two opposite characters such as a noisy boy and a quiet girl, a giant elephant and a tiny mouse, and a good caterpillar and a bad slug.
- *The Hare and the Tortoise:* Act out the story using as many opposites as possible.

Role-play

Two opposite areas, e.g. hot and cold
Set up: Hot area: use a yellow mat for the sand, swimming costumes, sun hats, sun glasses, sun-cream, beach towels, buckets and spades, a blue mat for the seawater, a cold snack of ice-creams and iced drinks. Cold area: use a white mat for the snow, Wellington boots, scarves, hats, gloves, mittens, skis, soft-toy polar bears, penguins, seals, a warm snack of cocoa and hot, buttered muffins.

Roles: Children, families, life-guards, holiday makers, polar explorers, Inuits etc.

Stories: In the hot aread reenact a family holiday on the beach; learning to swim; safe sun-bathing; a lost child on the beach; a sand-carving competition. Then in the cold area get children to explore the North pole, walk in the snow, and build a snowman.

Stories

 Opposites by Nick Butterworth
Draw and paint pictures of opposites on folded sugar paper.

 The Little Red Ant and the Great Big Crumb by Shirley Climo
Act out the story as little red ant tries to move the big crumb.

 Mary Mary Quite Contrary by Judith Harries
Act out the story. Can the children think of any more opposites for Mary to try?

Mary Mary Quite Contrary
Mary was very contrary.

When mum said, "please can you fetch me a big plate?", Mary did the opposite and brought a small one!

When mum said, "please be quiet Mary, your baby sister is asleep," Mary did the opposite and made lots of noise!

When dad said, "Mary, we must walk to school quickly to meet your brother," Mary did the opposite and walked really slowly!
Mum would sigh and say "Mary Mary quite contrary!" and then one day they made a plan. That night mum and dad offered to read Mary a really long bedtime story. Mary, as always, wanted the opposite. Until she thought of all the tales she would be missing…

Songs and rhymes

- Jack And Jill Went Up The Hill
- The Grand Old Duke of York

- Hickory Dickory Dock
- Goosey Goosey Gander

Opposites Song

(Tune: If You're Happy And You Know It)
If you're happy and you know it, clap your hands…
If you're sad and you know it, pull a face…
If you're hot and you know it, wipe your brow…
If you're cold and you know it, shiver alot…
If you're tall and you know it, touch the sky…
If you're short and you know it, touch the floor…

Opposites Rap

Big and small, short and tall, finding the opposites rap
High and low, fast and slow, end it with a clap.
Hot and cold, new and old, more of them we've found
Fat and thin, out and in, lots of them around
Happy and sad, good and bad, finding the opposites rap
Black and white, day and night, end it with a clap.

> ## Design, Art and Modelling

Pencils and pens

- *Happy and sad faces:* Use felt pens to draw happy and sad faces on both sides of a wooden spoon. Add appropriate hair and clothes.
- *Thick and thin:* Provide a range of drawing media: thin pencils, fineliners and felt tips, thick marker pens, wax

crayons and chalks. How many different ways can the children make thick and thin lines? Try again with long and short lines.

Paint and print

- *Big and small painting:* Try using big sheets of paper on an easel with big household paintbrushes or tiny pieces of paper and tiny brushes.
- *Top and bottom of it:* Stick paper to the top and underside of a table and have fun painting on both surfaces. Invite children to lie on the floor and paint above their heads.

Collage

- *Black and white:* Cut up black and white paper to make opposite collages. Stick white shapes onto black paper and vice versa. Are the patterns symmetrical?
- *Shadow art:* Use an overhead projector or torch as a source of light. Ask child to place their hand in between the light and the wall so it casts a shadow. Draw round the shadow onto a piece of paper. Cut out two copies, one in white, one in black and display on the opposite colours. Try with different objects.

Modelling

- *Weaving:* Help children to make holes all round the sides of a shallow box or lid and thread wool through to make

a weaving frame. Weave strips of ribbon, fabric, feathers, lace, string, wool and paper in and out, up and down, etc.

Clay and dough

- *Soft and hard:* Observe and talk about the differences between handling soft playdough and firmer plasticine and clay. Make some salt and flour dough and use to make different shapes in a variety of thicknesses. Look at some different opposites such as long and short, fat and thin, straight and wavy, whole and broken. Bake the shapes and notice how the dough goes harder when cooked.

Famous Art

Bridget Riley - Metamorphosis
Spotty opposites: Experiment with circular printing tools: bottle tops, yoghurt pots, sponges, finger tips, etc. to create black spots on a white background and/or white spots on a black background.

Dance and Movement

Warm Up

In the style of the game Jumping Beans a chosen leader calls out actions and their subsequent opposite e.g. jumping beans fast, jumping beans slow, frozen beans tall, frozen beans small, broad beans and narrow beans, runner beans fast, runner beans slow and so on. Encourage the children to create their own moves to match the actions.

Dance

The Grand Old Duke of York
March around the room encouraging the children to recognise the opposite movements

Up the hill- stretching up tall and walking on tip toes
Down the hill – crouching down low

Try marching and singing quietly then repeat loudly. How about marching forwards and then backwards? How many more opposites can the children think of? Instruments can add another dimension to the dance.

Musical bumps / statues
Play these games and emphasise the opposite movements of up and down, standing and sitting or moving about and standing perfectly still.

Movement games

Over and under
With the children, create an obstacle course that encourages the children to move over and under different challenges – over some stepping stones, under a sheet, over some tyres, under a chair and so on.

Cool Down

Parachute faces
Sitting in a circle around the edge of the parachute invite children to hold the fabric up in front of their faces. Call out a feeling, the fabric is lowered and the children's expressions are revealed. As their confidence builds encourage them to pull a face opposite to the feeling called out.

Ourselves

Drama games

- *Catch my name:* Sit in a circle and say your name. Then throw a bean bag or soft toy to a child. They say their name and then throw to another child. Continue until everyone has had a turn.
- *Name game:* Go round the circle helping the children to invent alliterative names for themselves such as Jumpy John, Angry Adam, Moaning Megan, Happy Harriet and ask them to make up an action to go with their new name.
- *Head to toe:* This is a riotous warm up game. Ask children to move carefully around the room. Shout out two body parts e.g. knees and head, and the children must join their knee to someone else's head as soon as possible!

Mime

- *Throw that feeling:* See the mime game suggested in the topic of Friends.
- *What's my line:* Talk about different jobs that the children's parents, families and friends do. Invite them to mime a job for the others to guess. See also the topics of Night and Growth.
- *Mirrors:* Work with a partner and point to different parts of the face, body etc. as the mirror tries to copy. Sing 'head, shoulders, knees and toes' for the mirror to copy. See activities suggested in the topics of Food and Opposites.

Drama skills

- Improvise a drama in a film or photographic studio. Talk about the characters: the camera operator, sound man, make-up artist, director, actors, agents, and so on. Record a popular current advertisement from the television or a traditional story. What could go wrong during the filming?

Role-play

Doctor's or dentist's surgery

Set up: Doctor's surgery – nurse's uniform, white coats, doctor's kit, stethoscope, prescription pad, phone, diary, computer, posters about keeping healthy, empty pill bottles, bandages, sling, pretend casts, wheelchair. Dentist's surgery - uniforms, a special chair, bib, toothbrushes, charts showing teeth and how to look after them. A waiting room with magazines, comfy chairs and reception area.

Roles: Doctor, nurse, dentist, receptionist, patients.

Stories: Go into the doctor's groaning and in pain, keep telling the doctor a different part of your body hurts; the first visit to the dentist; a doctor can't work out what is wrong with the patient.

Stories

Funnybones by Allan Ahlberg
Cut and stick white art straws to create skeletons on black sugar paper.

We've All Got Belly Buttons by David Martin
Draw around a child's body on a large sheet of paper and paint on clothes and a face. Add labels for all the body parts from the book.

When An Elephant Comes To School by Jan Ormerod
Ask children to remember how they felt on their first day at school and act it out.

Rumpelstiltskin Traditional
Play a circle game with the children's names. Clap two times slowly, and then pause for two counts. Ask children to take turns around the circle to say or sing their name in the gap.

Songs and rhymes

- Heads, Shoulders, Knees And Toes
- One Finger, One Thumb, Keep Moving
- If You're Happy And You Know It
- Round And Round The Garden
- Oliver Twist, You Can't Do This

There's Lots of Bones In Me!
(Tune: There Are No Strings On Me from Pinnochio*)*
I've got two eyes, a mouth and nose,
Ten little fingers and ten little toes.

I've got two legs and two strong arms,
There's lots of bones in me!

I've got two hands, a neck and chin,
And lots of skin to keep them in.
I've got a spine, a skull and ribs,
There's lots of bones in me!

Tickling rhymes
(Tune: Round And Round The Garden)
Up and down the hillside
(Tickle up and down arms)
Run the naughty ants
Up and down, round and round
(Tickle up and down, round and round)
And into your pants.
(End with pat on the bottom)

Hello!
(Tune: Here I Come)

Leader	Response
Hello!	Hello
What's your name?	(insert child's name)
Where are you from?	(insert home town)
Well done!	Well done!
Bonjour	Bonjour
Guten Tag	Guten Tag
Say shalom	Say shalom
Well done!	Well done!

Design, Art and Modelling

Pencils and pens

- *Mirror images:* Ask children to look in hand mirrors and draw or sketch self-portraits. Start with head and shoulders and then try full body portraits.
- *Chalk pictures:* Use white and coloured chalk to draw body shapes on the pavement and playground. The children can draw around each other in different positions rather like the 'scene of a crime'!

Paint and print

- *Life-size portrait:* Choose a volunteer to lie down on a large piece of paper and draw round the outline. Draw in the facial features and use paint to decorate the body

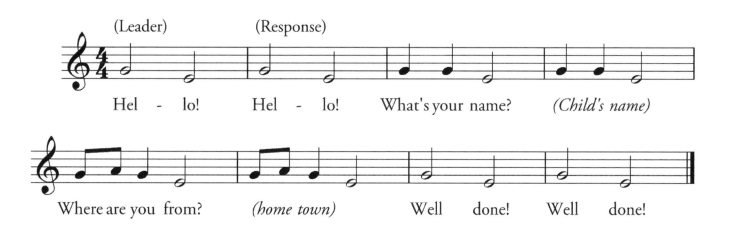

shape with clothes. Display the portrait and add labels for the different body parts.

- *Aboriginal hand prints:* Draw round hands and cut out of paper. Tape the shape onto some black paper and then squirt or flick white and red paint around the hand. Remove the cut out and see the hand print that remains.

Collage

- *Skeletons:* Cut pieces of white art straws and arrange into the shape of a human skeleton. Stick onto black sugar paper. Try skeletons of other animals.
- *Me masks:* Cut out simple face shapes or masks from coloured paper using a template (see templates at the back of this book). Fold paper to create nose and ears and attach with staples. Cut and curl paper to make eyelashes and hair.

Modelling

- *Outdoor rockface:* Use found materials to create a face, for instance, stones for eyes, grass and feathers for hair, and moss for a mouth. Take photographs.

Clay and dough

- *Hand prints:* Show children how to make a clay hand print by pressing their hand onto a rounded piece of clay. Add a felt base and give to parents as a keepsake!

Famous Art

Henri Matisse – Portrait of Lydia

Block colour portraits: Invite children to paint themselves in the style of Matisse. Use solid black lines as an outline and fill in with bold primary colours.

Dance and Movement

Warm Up

 How many different ways can the children move the different parts of their bodies? For example;

Feet – stamping, marching, kicking, hopping, tapping and tip toes

Hands – clapping, waving, pointing, banging plus any of the simple signing children may know

Name a part of the body and let the children do the rest.

Dance

The following songs and dances are ideal for this topic; The Hokey Cokey; Head, Shoulders, Knees and Toes; One Finger One Thumb; If You're Happy and You Know It; Looby Loo and Them Bones Them Bones.

Shadow dances

On a sunny day take the children's favourite music outdoors and let them dance about noticing their shadows as they move. Encourage the children to see how high or how small, how wide or how narrow they can make their shadows. Give the children chalk so they can draw around each other's shadows.

Movement Games

Two Together

Call out two body parts. The children attempt to join these parts as one. For example leg and hand, tummy and knee or elbow and hip. Calling out impossible combinations such as head and tummy will help children to understand the limitations of their bodies. Invite children to take turns in calling out the body parts.

Body Band

Make music using only body parts – feet stamping, hands clapping, fingers snapping, tongue clicking, and mouths popping and so on. Move around the room as a marching band whilst you make music.

Cool Down

Ask the children to sit as a group on the floor. Explain that the object of the activity is to form the first letter of their name using their body. How many more letters can they make with their bodies? They can sit, stand or lie on the floor.

Patterns

Drama and Role Play

Drama games

- *Sound circle:* Sit in a circle and choose two or three body sounds to create a repeating pattern, for instance 'clap, tap knees, clap tap knees'. Pass the pattern around the circle. Try again with vocal sounds such as 'tick, ss, wow'.
- *Echo clapping and singing:* Clap a simple rhythm pattern and invite children to echo you. When they are confident ask for volunteers to lead and clap the patterns. Try singing a simple two-note pattern based on the cuckoo call and invite the children to echo.

Mime

- *Body patterns:* Ask children to work with a partner. Stand facing each other and create patterns such as stretch up, crouch down, clap hands, turn around. Can they make up their own pattern and demonstrate it to the group?
- *Letter shapes:* Ask pairs of children to use their bodies to create the shapes of their initials. Remind them that they can stand up, sit down or lie on the floor. Try again with numbers.

Drama skills

- Create some physical drama with the whole group. Make patterns using children's bodies. Ask children to work with a partner to create an arch. Use shapes to create a zigzag across the room. Ask children to stand in rows and stretch arms and legs wide. What other patterns can the children make with their bodies?

Role-play

Art gallery

Set up: Mount and display lots of artwork showing patterns done by the children or artists. Patterned wallpaper, patterned posters and tickets, a ticket office with a phone, computer, cash till, money, wrapping paper and bags. Make a catalogue for the gallery containing the names of the paintings, artists and prices.

Roles: Visitors, sales assistant, artists, manager.

Stories: Opening night of a new show at the gallery; a very nervous artist; a valuable work of art is stolen; a competition to choose the best patterned artwork; a gallery is under threat of closure; a rude visitor doesn't appreciate the show.

Stories, Songs and Rhymes

Stories

My Mum And Dad Make Me Laugh by Nick Sharatt
Design spotty clothes for mum and stripey clothes for dad.

How The Leopard Got His Spots by Rudyard Kipling
Research and paint animal patterns.

Who Are You, Stripy Horse? by Jim Helmore
Create patterned and collage pictures in the style of the book.

A Bad Case Of Stripes by David Shannon
Get the children to make colourful stripey self-portraits of themselves.

Up and down, up and down, stretch and bend, stretch and bend,

Tall and small, Tall and small, Let's make a bo - dy pat - tern.

Songs and rhymes

Patchwork Quilt

(Tune: This old man)
Patchwork quilt
Matching squares
Each one sewn together with care.
Stripes and flowers and rows of dots
What a lot of patterns we've got!

Patchwork quilt
Matching squares
Each one makes me want to stare
Red and yellow and orange too
Such a lot of patterns for you.

Let's Make A Pattern

(Tune: original)
Up and down, up and down,
Stretch and bend, stretch and bend,
Tall and small, tall and small,
Let's make a body pattern.

Stamp and clap, stamp and clap,
Click and tap, click and tap,
Pop and slap, pop and slap,
Let's make a noisy pattern.

Design, Art and Modelling

Pencils and pens

- *Squared paper animals:* Use squared or graph paper and choose a sequence of colours to create a repeated colour pattern. Draw round animal stencils to create Elmer the elephant and his friends (see templates at the back of this book).
- *Mendhi patterns:* Draw around hands and design some Indian mendhi patterns using felt pens. Ask children to experiment by making the mendhi patterns on their own hands and feet using washable brown felt pen or paint and cotton wool buds. Is it easier to paint each other's hands? How does it feel? Does it tickle?

Paint and print

- *Cotton-reel rollers:* Push a pencil through an empty cotton reel. Cover the reel with a thick layer of plasticine. Press a pattern of shapes into the plasticine using the blunt end of a pencil. Roll the reel in paint and then onto paper.
- *Glass painting:* Draw outlines of shapes and patterns onto a small glass. Fill shapes in with different colours. Use as a tea light holder.

Collage

- *Mobile rangoli:* Provide lots of different materials such as seeds, rice, cereals, coconut, sand, mixed with powder paint or food dye for colour. Make the patterns on strong pieces of card and place them on the floor or in doorways. Apply glue in the required shape and then sprinkle the dry materials on top.
- *Mosaic:* Make mosaic patterns using tiny squares of coloured plastic, card or broken tiles.

Modelling

- *Spiral decorations:* Cut out circles of card or foil and colour or paint patterns onto them on both sides. Help children to carefully cut in a spiral and stretch out. Hang from a string to decorate the room.

Clay and dough

- *Pattern tiles:* Roll out clay to a thickness of 5mm and cut into a square tile. Divide the tile into four smaller squares and then use clay tools to decorate each part with repeated patterns. Try zigzags, spots, stripes and wavy lines.

Stepping  Stones to Creativity

Famous Art

Aboriginal art
– www.aboriginalartonline.com

Aboriginal dot art: Look at some different examples of traditional and contemporary aboriginal art with the children. Take a thick felt pen for a walk all over a piece of paper making shapes and swirls. Use cotton buds and earthy coloured paints such as brown, red, orange and black and fill in with dots.

Dance and Movement

Warm Up

Clap Tap a Rhythm
Clap or tap a rhythm for the children to copy. Repeat and gradually build the rhythm to something more complicated. As the children become more confident invite them to clap or tap out rhythms for the other children to copy.

Clapping names
Take it in turns to clap out your names using a clap for each syllable. For example Heather would be 'Heath' (one clap), 'Er' (one clap), Christopher would be 'Chris' (one clap) 'To' (one clap) 'Pher' (one clap). Who has the most claps in their name and who has the least? You can vary this activity by tapping out names using different parts of your body.

Dance

Line Dancing
Line dancing is an excellent introduction for patterns in dance. Use the lively music to make up simple routines using some classic line dancing steps such as holding hands on hips whilst you tap your feet, pretending to twirl your lasso or clap your hands together then slap your thighs. Giving the children dressing up props such as cow boy hats and boots can encourage further enthusiasm and fun.

Movement Games

Patterns
Mark out areas on the ground in chalk. Give the children pieces of chalk and invite them to create patterns within the marked areas such as spots, zig zags, stripes, swirls or any pattern they can think of. Once the areas have been marked, gather the children in the centre. The aim off the game is then to call out a pattern and the children run to the corresponding area as quickly as possible. Vary the activity by calling out different ways of moving to the pattern called e.g. hopping, skipping or jumping.

Cool Down

Sitting quietly as a group think of slow controlled movements you can perform together. Create a pattern as you do so such as two deep breaths in, one stretch down to your toes, two deep breaths in and one final stretch down to your toes. What other combinations can the children create?

Pets

Drama and Role Play

Drama games

● *Introductions:* Sit in a circle and take turns to introduce yourself and then talk to the group about your pet. For example 'my name is Judith and I have two cats called Smudge and Ronnie and a rabbit called Flopsy.' See also the topic of Colours.

Mime

● What's my pet? Choose different pets to look after in a mime: take your dog for a walk or throw a ball for it to fetch; stroke the cat; play with the hamster in its wheel or ball; let your mouse run from hand to hand; feed your bird. Can anyone guess what sort of pet you have?

Drama skills

● Improvise a drama about a new pet, for instance 'the snuffletoise'. You are asked to look after this new pet for someone. Describe it and its needs. Agree to look after it, nervously, and do your best. Resolve the drama by pretending that an alien turns up to ask for his snuffletoise back!

● *The lost pet:* Ask the children to work with a partner and create a poster about a lost pet. Take turns to phone the police to report the lost pet. Ask them to sit back to back with one playing the owner and the other the police officer.

Role-play

A pet shop

Set up: Soft-toy animals, baskets, cages made from flexible, plastic straws or cut-out boxes, magnetic fish, pet food, cash till, money, posters, pet toys, hutches, collars, name tags etc. Make home-made hamsters by stuffing tights with buttons sewn-on for eyes.

Roles: Petshop owner, sales assistant, customers, pets, animal breeder.

Stories: A rare animal escapes in the shop; an awkward customer can't decide which pet to buy; a best-in-show pet competition; buying a new kitten.

Stories, Songs and Rhymes

Stories

 I Want A Pet by Lauren Child
Design your own perfect pet that nobody in the family will object to.

 I Wish I Were A Dog by Lydia Monks
Use the vibrant colour illustrations to inspire children to paint pictures of their own pets.

 I Want a Cat by Tony Ross
Act out the story

 That Pesky Rat by Lauren Child
Use black sugar paper and coloured tissue paper to make a cityscape of buildings in the style of the book. Glue a cut-out rat in front of the cityscape.

Songs and rhymes

● Pussy Cat, Pussy Cat
● I Love Little Pussy
● Ding Dong Bell
● How Much Is That Doggie In The Window?

My poor-ly pet needs to see the vet, My poor-ly pet needs to see the vet,

My poor-ly pet needs to see the vet, He has hurt his paw.

My Poorly Pet
(Tune: original)
My poorly pet needs to see the vet X3
He has hurt his _____
*Insert different parts of pet such as tail, leg, head, ear,
fin, paw, etc.*

Please Be My Pet
(Tune: Pease Pudding Hot)
Please be my pet
Sweet pussy cat
I will look after you
Fancy that!

Please be my pet
Fine puppy dog
I will look after you
Go for a jog!

Please be my pet
Brown guinea pig
I will look after you
Dance a jig!

Hippety Hop To The Pet Shop
(Tune: Hippety Hop to the Candy Shop)
Hippety hop to the pet shop
To buy a pet for Mary
Try a cat, perhaps a fish,
Or even a canary.

Hippety hop to the pet shop
To buy a pet for Peter.
Try a dog, perhaps a snake
Or better still a cheetah!

*Try making up your own verses using children's names and
different pets.*

Design, Art and Modelling

Pencils and pens

- *Pet photographs:* Ask children to bring in photographs of their pets or a pet they would like to own. Make black and white sketches of the photographs. In a group use the photos and drawings to create a pet collage.

Paint and print

- *Portraits from life:* Arrange for children to bring their pets into the setting and sketch the animals. Turn the sketches into paintings. Discuss how brush techniques could be used to show fur, whiskers, feathers, etc.

Collage

- *Birds of paradise:* Cut simple bird shapes from thin card using templates (see templates at the back of this book). Use brightly coloured tissue and sugar paper to cut, curl, fringe and concertina beautiful feathers. Arrange and secure the feathers, add a beak, eyes and feet. Hang on string suspended across the room.

Modelling

- *Sock hamsters:* Make a small friendly pet! Stuff small white, grey, brown or black socks with tights, cotton wool, sponge, etc. Secure the end of the sock by tying a knot, fastening with an elastic band or sewing. Add buttons for eyes and a felt nose. Try naming the mini-pets!
- *Perfect pets:* Provide dry pasta tubes, beads, buttons, pompoms and pipe cleaners. Thread, twist and stick together the perfect pet. How many legs, wings, and feet will it have?

Clay and dough

- *Salt dough pets:* Ask children to choose a favourite pet and cut circular shapes from dough to make its face. Affix ears, a nose, eyes and whiskers. Use clay tools, garlic press, cutlery, etc. to create that furry face! Bake and paint.
- *Caged pets:* Use playdough and cocktail sticks or matchsticks to build cages for tiny pets.

Famous Art

Edouard Manet
- Le Rendezvous des Chats

Black & white cats: Observe the two cats in the picture. What are they doing? Discuss the shapes of their bodies and tails. Cut different cat shapes (see templates at the back of this book) from black sugar paper and stick onto a roof drawn in pencil or cut out of corrugated cardboard.

Dance and Movement

Warm Up

Mime pet animals
Suggestions:
A dog – on all fours wagging your behind as a tail
A goldfish – wide open mouths opening and shutting
A duck or a chicken – waddling and flapping wings
A cat – stretching and cleaning paws
A snake – sliding gracefully
A rabbit – hopping

Dance

Create dance for the following verses to the tune of *The Wheels on the Bus*;

The dogs in the park run all around
The cats on the wall are fast asleep
The fish in the pond swim up and down
The parrots in the cage are squawking very loud
Can the children think of any other verses?

♪ An aquarium dance
You will need a copy of the popular piece of music "Under the Sea" from the Walt Disney film, *The Little Mermaid*. Simply provide children with a clear open space to dance and move about as if they were fish in an aquarium.

Movement Games

Throw and fetch
Pretend to be dogs in the park enjoying a game of fetch. One child is a dog owner throwing the ball to another child who is the dog. Give the children bouncy balls to use whilst they play.

Cats on the wall
Use low level beams to provide a pretend wall. Imagine you are a cat walking along the wall. Can you reach the end without falling off?

Cool down

Imagine you are a chosen tired pet. Clean yourself then stretch and yawn before settling down for a well earned rest.

Stepping Stones to Creativity

Pirates

Drama games

- *What's the time Captain Hook?:* Play this game in the style of 'what's the time Mr Wolf?' Choose a child to be Captain Hook and stand facing away from the rest of the children. They all chant the question and he replies with a time such as 'three o'clock', and the others all take three steps nearer to him. The aim is to get close enough to touch Captain Hook without him catching you. If he calls 'it's time to walk the plank' he is allowed to turn around and try to catch a child to take his place.

Mime

- *Walking the plank:* Give each child and yourself a folded-up piece of paper. First time round make sure that you get the paper with a black spot marked on and have to walk the plank. Mime being scared as you walk along a narrow plank of wood and then jump into the deep water. Play again and let some of the children walk the plank.

Drama skills

- Help the children to draw treasure maps on squared paper with an X marking the spot where the treasure is hidden. Improvise a drama about searching for treasure on an island. Talk about the different characters that might be looking for the same treasure. Will the pirates co-operate with each other? What happens when they find the treasure?

Role-play

A pirate ship

Set up: Use wooden bricks, soft building bricks or a climbing frame to create a pirate ship. Add ladders for climbing on board and a balance beam for a plank to walk along. Use hoops or old tyres as port holes. Hang up a large sheet for the sail and add ropes and string. Point out any hazards and explain to the children that they will have to be very careful not to trip when playing on the pirate ship.

Roles: Pirates, sailors, mermaids, Captain Hook, Captain Jack Sparrow, prisoners.

Stories: Talk to the children about any pirate stories they are already familiar with that could be role played in the pirate ship. Sail to a treasure island, chase another ship, make someone walk the plank, run out of healthy food at sea.

Stories

The Lighthouse Keeper's Breakfast by Ronda Armitage
Dress up as pirates and act out the story.

The Night Pirates by Peter Harris
Cut out different papers to create pictures of the pirate ship and houses in the style of the book.

Tiny Ted and the Pirates by Ian Whybrow
Act out the story.

Pirate Pete by Kim Kennedy
Draw an annotated treasure map.

Captain Flinn and the Pirate Dinosaurs by Giles Andreae
Paint a picture of each child's favourite pirate dinosaur.

Songs and rhymes

- What Shall We Do With The Drunken Sailor?

We're Going On A Treasure Hunt
(Tune: We're Going On A Bear Hunt)
We're going on a treasure hunt,
We're going to find some treasure.
What a beautiful day.
We're not scared.
Uh oh!
Sinking sand!
We can't go over it
We can't go under it
We've got to go through it.
Squelch, squelch, squelch!
Sharp rough rocks – climb, trip, scratch…
Deep cold water – splash, splash, splash…
Dark damp cave – creep, creep, creep…
What's inside?

Is it the treasure?
It's got feathers and a sharp beak.
Screech, screech, screech…

Run to safety backwards through the rhyme.

Looking For Treasure

Looking for treasure
Searching for jewels
Reading the map
Following the rules
X marks the spot
Where treasure was hid
Stepping the trail
As the pirates did.

The Treasure's All For Me

(Tune: A Sailor Went To Sea)
A pirate went to sea, sea, sea,
To see what he could see, see, see,
But all that he could see, see, see,
Was the bottom of the deep blue sea, sea, sea.

He dived down through the sea, sea, sea,
And found a rusty key, key, key,
He shouted out with glee, glee, glee
'The treasure's all for me, me, me!'

Design, Art and Modelling

Pencils and pens

- *Treasure map:* Draw the outline shape of an island. Add trees, houses, mountains, water and of course an 'x' to mark the spot where the treasure is hidden. Help children to carefully burn the edges of the map to make it look old and well travelled!
- *Quill pens:* Provide large feathers and ink and let the children try to draw and write using old-fashioned quills. Can they write a secret message to some fellow pirates?

Paint and print

- *Skull and crossbones:* Make flags by using white paint to paint the shape of the traditional 'Jolly Roger' skull and crossbones on to a black sugar paper rectangle. Alternatively, fold the paper into a pirate's hat. Don't forget to make an eye patch too!
- *Walk the plank:* Use bare feet to make watery footprints on some paper or ground. Invite children to jump out of a shallow tray of water to make a big splashy puddle shape.

- *Pretty Polly:* Use lots of bright colours to paint a parrot for a friendly pirate. Add a few feathers. Can the parrot talk?

Collage

- *Pirate ships:* Paint a watery background using thin blue and green paint combed into a rough sea. Stick on a ship shape cut out of corrugated cardboard. Use string and triangles of cotton fabric to create sails and rigging.

Modelling

- *Treasure chests:* Use boxes with hinged lids such as tea bags or shoe boxes, or a cereal box with a lid cut out on three sides. Cover in pva glue and stick on shiny paper to create a sparkly decoupage effect. Fill with doubloons made from plastic lids covered in shiny paper.
- *Model pirate ship:* Use large cardboard boxes, wooden bricks, broom handles or dowelling, and sheets to construct a giant model ship. Dress up as pirates and pose on the top for photos.

Clay and dough

- *Pressed coins:* Roll salt dough out very thinly and cut out circles using biscuit cutters or plastic lids. Press coins into the dough circles or make your own designs for pirate money. Bake, paint and spend.

Famous Art

Disney's Peter Pan
Captain Hook's pirate ship: Paint a big picture of a pirate ship.

Cut out pictures of the characters from a magazine or poster and arrange on the ship.

Dance and Movement

Warm Up

Pretend to be pirates preparing your ship to set sail. Get out the brooms and clear the deck with long sweeping motions. On your hands and knees, scrub the deck with wide circular motions. Imagine you are pulling up the sails using long heavy ropes. Can the children think of any other jobs that need doing before you begin the voyage?

Dance

All Aboard

You will need a copy of "He's a Pirate" from the film The Pirates of the Caribbean: The Curse of the Black Pearl. This dramatic music is ideal for performing your journey across the seas. Encourage the children to imagine rowing the gigantic heavy oars. Who will steer the ship its course? Who will climb the rigging to keep look out? Are there any enemy ships coming? Do you need to get out the cannons?

Yo, Ho!

You arrive at a desert island. Dancing along to "Yo Ho!", make believe you are searching for treasure marked on an imaginary map. The music lends itself perfectly for such a dance.

Movement Games

In the sea and on the shore

Lay a rope on the floor. Ask all the children to stand on one side of the rope – this is the side of the shore / the beach.

Explain the other side is the sea.

When the leader calls out "In the sea" all the children must jump over the rope into the sea. When the leader calls out "on the shore" they must all jump back again. Start slowly and then get faster and faster. Try to catch the children out by calling the same instruction twice!

Pirates Ship

In a long open space designate an end to be the PORT side and an end to be the STARBOARD side. A child is chosen to be Captain. The other children are pirates. Captain is given a hand bell or a drum. When Captain calls our PORT or STARBOARD the pirates run quickly to that end of the room. If the Captain shakes his bell or bangs his drum all pirates must pretend to climb the rigging. Change the Captain frequently to allow all children a turn. For older children when PORT or STARBOARD is called you can add a way of moving e.g. PORT jump and all pirates must jump to PORT or STARBOARD hop and all pirates must hop to STARBOARD.

Cool Down

Imagine you are tired pirates getting into your hammocks for a sleep. Before you rest your heads you are going to stretch your tired limbs. With legs outstretched bend forward and touch your toes. Who can get their head on their knees? Stretch arms up tall and then out wide – pretending to yawn as you do so. Just before you go to sleep tell the other pirates about your favourite part of the day's adventures.

Puppets

Drama and Role Play

Drama games

- *My friend Albert…:* Take along a large hand puppet, preferably with a moving mouth, and introduce it to the children. It doesn't have to be called Albert! Help them to befriend the puppet and gain confidence so they can speak to it without embarrassment. Use the puppet at each drama session to introduce new ideas and challenges. Children sometimes find it easier to relate to a puppet than they do a new adult.
- Make a collection of finger or hand puppets and let each child choose one to use. Make your puppet speak to the group. Take turns for children to introduce their puppet to the group. Ask them to choose a partner and invite their puppets to have a conversation.

Mime

- *Come to life:* Ask the children to find a space in the room and stand still like a puppet made of wood, plastic or fabric. On an agreed signal ask them to slowly 'come to life'. Practise this transformation gradually with each part of the puppet slowly tingling, then wiggling, then moving more purposefully until the puppets are dancing.
- *Teaching Albert:* Choose an activity and mime instructions for the puppet Albert (see above) to follow such as making biscuits, getting ready for bed, or buying a new pair of shoes.

Drama skills

- *Home-made puppets:* Encourage children to make their own simple finger puppets from paper or felt and to improvise dramas and stories using them in a small group.
- *Pinnochio:* Talk about the story of Pinnochio. Relate this to the mime game 'come to life' above. Act out parts of the story.

Role-play

A puppet show

Set up: Lots of different puppets, a mini-theatre made from a large cardboard box with the front cut out and a curtain added.

Alternatively, hang up a sheet or curtain over a washing line and let the children stand behind and hold the puppets up over the top.

Roles: Puppeteers, audience, ticket sellers, programme designers etc.

Stories: Use puppets to tell any traditional story or improvise new ones. Puppets could get lost or start to misbehave; a noisy audience heckling; the show starts late, or the curtain won't open, and so on.

Stories, Songs and Rhymes

Stories

Pinnochio Traditional
Act out scenes from the story when the puppet comes to life.

I'm A Little Monkey by Tim Weave
Make felt finger puppets of Monkey's animal friends.

 Cheeky Monkey! by Mel Astill
Act out the story of Joe and his puppet Jojo.

Cheeky Monkey!

There were teddies in Joe's toy box, a wooden fire engine, a dance mat and some animal puppets. The teddies were cuddled and taken for picnics, the fire engine was raced to emergencies and the dance mat was danced upon until Joe's feet were sore...but no-one ever played with the puppets.

Joe wasn't careful with his toys. Teddy's leg had fallen off, there were two wheels missing from the fire engine and the dance mat had been stamped upon a bit too hard. "I'm bored!" shouted Joe, "I've got NOTHING to play with!" Joe's mum looked in his toy box, "what about your puppets?" "BORING!" yelled Joe. "That's all there is that isn't broken," said mum sadly.

Joe sat and thought. He peered into the toy box and pulled out a monkey puppet. He made the monkey nod his head, wave his arms, clap his paws and swing around the room. Joe had an idea! He found mum reading a book so he made the puppet pop up above the book.

"Hello", said the puppet. "Hello" said mum. "I'm Jojo the monkey," said the puppet. "Hello Jojo" said mum. "I know a boy called Joe who is sorry for being cross, and not being careful with his toys" said the puppet. "That's good, I am glad" said mum. "Would you like a banana Jojo?" asked mum. "No...but I would!" said Joe leaping up and giving his mum a big hug. "Cheeky monkey!" laughed mum.

Songs and rhymes

- There Are No Strings On Me

Ten Finger Puppets

(Tune: Ten Little Indians)
There was one, there were two,
There were three finger puppets,
There were four, there were five,
There were six finger puppets,
There were seven, there were eight,
There were nine finger puppets,
Ten finger puppets on my hands.

I'm A Little Puppet

(Tune: I'm A Little Teapot)
I'm a little puppet, tall and thin
Here's my body and here's my strings.
When you pull the right one, I'll begin
To move and dance and even sing!

Design, Art and Modelling

Pencils and pens

- *Finger tip puppets:* Help children to cut the finger tips off yellow washing up gloves and draw faces on with permanent felt pens. Place on fingers to create an instant set of puppets. Make hats for the puppets using a small circle of thin card or felt cut and folded into a cone.

Paint and print

- *Pop-up puppets:* Draw or paint a face onto a small wooden spoon. Make clothes using material taped around the handle. Paint a cardboard tube and rest the spoon inside to pop up and down. Use to tell stories to each other or play peekaboo!

Collage

- *Walking finger puppets:* Use templates to cut a puppet shape out of cardboard (see templates at the back of this book). Help children to cut two finger holes in the base to poke fingers through. Can they make the puppet walk? Draw a face on the top of the card or cut and stick on pictures of people from magazines.

Modelling

- *Instant dragon finger puppet:* Cut off a finger from an old woolly glove and add beads for eyes, a felt nose and mouth, sequins for scales, and a fiery red tongue. What other characters could the children make using different types of gloves?
- *Sock puppets:* Provide some clean old socks. Sew or stick on buttons for eyes, leather or felt ears, spikes, tails, etc. Invite children to wear them on their hands and make them talk.

Clay and dough

- *Dough digits:* Try moulding a dough finger puppet around children's index fingers and then use tools to create a face. Make different characters and let them talk to each other.

Famous Art

Disney's Pinnochio

String puppet: Look at a real string puppet. Cut out shapes

of body, head, arms and legs and join with split pins. Attach strings to the ends of the arms and wrap around a piece of dowelling or a pencil. Can children make their puppets wave?

Oversized socks
Play as your would a three legged race using very large sock puppets to hold the children's legs together.

Dance and Movement

Warm Up

Take shoes off. Inform children that their socks are puppets and invite them to move their puppets about using their feet. Suggestions for movements – swing legs, march legs, stretch legs up high or out to the side. Then ask children to remove their puppets and place them onto another body part for moving such as their hands or their head.

Dance

Chinese dragon dance
The Chinese dragon is a very large puppet. Give the children large sheets of colourful fabric for them to line up under. Play traditional Chinese music and invite children to move about as dragons.

Shadow puppets
In a darkened room project a light onto a clear wall. Invite children to create shadows on the wall as if they were shadow puppets. They may choose to use only their arms and hands or they may choose to use their whole bodies. Playing different types of music will encourage very different types of movements.

Pinnochio
Attach lengths of ribbon to children's wrists and ankles before dancing along to Disney's *Pinnochio* music "I've got no strings".

Movement Games

Pantomime Horses
Children need to pair up for this game. One child is the front of the horse and the other is the rear of the horse. You can choose to race the horses against each other, complete obstacle courses or simply invite them to perform and dance along to chosen music.

Cool Down

Butterfly puppets
Sitting on the floor, place the soles of the feet together and bounce knees up and down to create a flying butterfly. Flutter arms up and down like a butterfly. Can children create a butterfly using their hands only?

Recycling

Drama games

- *Prop box:* Put together a collection of items that could be used as props such as a telephone, handbag, bunch of keys, plane tickets, wallet or purse, birthday card, newspaper, camera, torch, slipper, egg cup, sun cream etc. Put them all in a box and label it the 'prop box'. Invite children to take turns to pick an object from the box and think of a sentence or line of dialogue including the name of the object.

Mime

- *Pass the prop:* Sit in a circle and choose an item of junk to pass round. Each child has to mime using the 'junk' prop as though it was something else. Can anybody guess what they are pretending to use? Try using a cardboard tube, saucepan lid, wooden spoon, feather, aluminum foil tray etc. See the topic of Holes.

Drama skills

- *The story of a newspaper:* Talk about where paper comes from and trace the journey from a tree being chopped down, to a saw mill, to being flattened into pulp, being made into paper and printed on. Then finally being read and recycled. Help the children present the information in a drama showing each stage of the process.
- *Prop box dramas:* Extend the prop box game (see above) into improvised dramas. Ask a pair of children to each pick a prop by either design or chance and to make up a drama using them. Start with 'action' and ask them to stop when you say 'freeze'.

Role-play

Recycling centre/Second hand shop

Set up: Plastic boxes and bins labeled for newspaper, cardboard, drink cans and tins, clothes and shoes. Make a bottle bank from a huge cardboard box painted green with holes cut in and let the children drop empty plastic bottles into it. A broom to sweep up the mess. Dressing-up clothes and shoes in different sizes to sort.

Roles: Manager, customers, sorters, cleaner.

Stories: All the boxes are full, where will the rubbish go? A lazy customer puts the wrong things in each box; the recycling centre is threatened with closure, get the children to organise a campaign to save the centre via a demonstration and produce placards.

Stories

 Dinosaurs And All That Rubbish by Michael Foreman
Make collages out of junk.

 One World by Michael Foreman
Make a world in a bucket using shells, stones, seaweed and toy fish.

 Why Should I Recycle? by Jen Green
Use the information from the book to create posters to promote recycling.

 George Saves The World By Lunchtime by Jo Readman
Act out the story of George's efforts to recycle.

Yucketypoo by Jilly Henderson-Long
Design creatures from rubbish.

Songs and rhymes

- My Old Man's A Dustman

Wonderful Earth
(Tune: original)
We all live on a wonderful earth,
Full of plants and animals and people too.
Let's not spoil our wonderful earth,
So here are some things you can try to do.

Pick up your litter, recycle those cans.
Sort out your rubbish and make some plans
To re-use bags and recycle the news,
We can all help if only we choose.

Chorus
Walk to school, and ride your bikes.
Plant some trees and treasure the sights
Of forests and rivers where fish want to swim,
We can all help and we're going to win.

Recycle Rap
See a piece of litter, pick it up, pick it up,
See a piece of litter, pick it up, pick it up.
Cans in the can, bottles in the bank,
Plastic in the bin and paper in the sack.
Recycle, all you can, recycle, that's the plan,
Recycle, all you can, recycle, that's the plan!

Drop It In The Recycling
(Tune: My Old Man's A Dustman)
Turn a tree to paper.
Read it if you can.

Drop it in the recycling
And then you have a plan.
Drink from a plastic bottle.
Save it from the bins.
Drop it in the recycling
Along with glass and tins.
Lots of junk around you?
Look at it once more!
Drop it in the recycling
Don't leave it on the floor.

Design, Art and Modelling

Pencils and pens

- *Recycling wax crayons:* Help children to grate some old wax crayons and sprinkle onto a sheet of paper. Put more paper on top and use a warm iron to melt the wax and make fantastic patterns.
- *Pencil sharpenings:* Sharpen lots of different sizes, colours and types of pencils. Make a picture together using the shavings.

Paint and print

- *Marbling:* Fill a shallow tray with water. Drip marbling inks, artist's oil paints or left over glass paints onto the surface of the water and stir gently with a stick. Float a piece of thick cartridge paper on top of the tray for 30 seconds, remove and then leave to dry. The swirly patterns look like marble.
- *Print blocks:* Draw a simple shape, picture or pattern onto a small rectangle of thick card. Cut up old elastic bands into small pieces and stick around the outline of the picture. Add a handle to the other side and use as a printing block.
- *Litter prints:* Print using found objects such as bottle tops, plastic bags, chocolate trays, plastic pots and bottles, sweet wrappers, etc. Scrunch, fold and roll to paint and print.

Collage

- *Paper paper everywhere:* Make a collection of different papers – paper bags, wrapping paper, sugar paper, sweet wrappers, tissue, wallpaper, doilys, newspaper, magazines. Cut and tear into colourful 2D collage pictures.
- *Plastic pictures:* Help children to cut up different coloured plastic bottles into a variety of shapes. Use to create mosaic pictures and patterns.

Modelling

- *Junk modelling:* Encourage children to use all sorts of boxes and packaging to create imaginative models and sculptures.
- *Paper sculpture:* Help children to make a simple shape using garden wire. Try a circle, cross, chair or tree shape. Use lots of different papers folded, concertina, rolled into tubes, screwed up, curled around, and moulded around the frame.
- *Jeans bag:* Help children to cut up the leg of an old pair of jeans and sew, staple or stick into a bag. Stick or sew on buttons, sequins and beads.

Clay and dough

- *Found sculptures:* Press found objects into a clay ball to create a sculpture. Try natural objects such as pine cones, seeds, twigs, feathers, stones, leaves, or manmade objects such as bottle tops, plastic lids, litter, matchsticks, buttons and beads.

Famous Art

Andy Goldsworthy - Before the Mirror

Wire sculpture: Bend a metal coat hanger into a circle. Attach pipe cleaners, garden wire, twigs, straws, strips of card, rolled up twisted newspaper or magazines.

Dance and Movement

Warm Up

In the style of Simon says call out the following instructions for children to action;

"Bottles" Children stand tall with hands above head
"Paper" Children lie flat on the floor
"Aluminium" Children move about stiffly as if robots
"Tyres" Children spin round and round
"Clothing" Children sway side to side holding out their clothes

Can the children think of any more things that can be recycled and an action to match?

Dance

Cheerleaders

Create streamers or pom poms with old newspapers that the children tear into strips and attach at one end with ribbon or sticky tape. Then make up simple cheerleading

routines with the children. Ideal moves could include star jumps, high kicks, jumping, skipping and marching.

Junk Band

Create a musical band using recycled materials such as old plastic bottles filled with rice, pasta or lentils for shakers. Old biscuit tins for drums, cardboard tubes for trumpets and old cardboard boxes with rubber bands for guitars. Invite the children to put on a show for the other children and adults. Perhaps they would like to perform their favourite rhymes and songs. Alternatively sing along to "Old MacDonald had a Band" using the instruments you have made for the verses e.g.

"Old MacDonald had a band e i e i o
And in that band he had some shakers e i e i o"

Ten Green Bottles – an ideal song for this topic. Sing along to a children's CD or simply on your own. Having the bottles lined up as a visual prop enhances the activity. Alternatively invite ten children to pretend to be the bottles.

Movement games

Support the children in creating a ten pin bowling alley or a tin can alley using recycled plastic bottles, cans and old newspapers. Then sit back and watch the children play their new games.

Cool Down

With the children, create a xylophone from old bottles and coloured water. A funnel and a small jug will help children to fill the bottles independently. Give the children metal spoons ad invite them to create tunes using their xylophone.

Senses

Drama games

- *Long distance news:* Invite the children to take turns to share some news with the group. Line up all the children at one end of the room and ask them to project their news across the room to you. Encourage them to speak slowly, clearly and as loud as they can without shouting.
- *Chinese whispers:* Sit in a circle and pass a secret message around the ring. Does the message get through unchanged?
- *Feelie bag:* Show children your prop bag and a collection of useful props. Put a prop in a cloth bag and ask a child to describe it to the group by touch only.

Mime

- *Blind pairs:* See the topic of Light.
- *Which sense?:* Mime different sensory activities for the group to guess such as smelling a flower, eating food, looking at a picture, listening to music, stroking a soft toy.
- *Nice and nasty smells:* Ask children to stand up tall and practice breathing in and out. See the activity in the topic of Growth. As they breathe in ask them to mime smelling nice smells such as flowers, perfume, chocolate, cookies, and fresh bread, or nasty smells such as mouldy cheese, dirty socks, manure, wet dogs etc.

Drama skills

- Improvise a drama about a group of children who have one of their senses highly developed, i.e. one can see things happening miles away, the other can hear sounds from a great distance. How could they help each other and other people?

Role-play

An opticians

Set up: Swivel chair, eye charts, lots of glasses frames, mirrors, coloured lights or torches, a waiting area, posters, brochures, magazines, a receptionist, computer, diary, phone. Make your own eye-charts using shapes, numbers and some letters.

Roles: Optician, receptionist, patients.

Stories: A patient is worried about not being able to see properly; a fussy customer can't decide which glasses suit her.

Stories

Lucy's Picture by Nicola Moon
Use a variety of textured materials to create a collage like Lucy does.

Who's Making That Smell/Noise? by Philip Hawthorn
Make a lift-the-flap picture of a favourite smell or sound.

The Gingerbread Man Traditional
Create a dance with the repeated phrase 'you can't catch me, I'm the gingerbread man' to chant as an accompaniment.

The Princess And The Pea Traditional
Act out the story. How dramatic can the princess be, as she can't sleep due to a pea under her mattress?

Songs and rhymes

- Heads, Shoulders, Knees And Toes

In My Own Way
(Tune: Oh When The Saints)
What can I see? X2
What can I see in school today?
I'm gonna make a list of sights
That I can see in school today.
Hear, smell, taste, feel, sounds, smells, tastes, touches…

What can I see? X2
What can I see at home today?
I'm gonna make a list of sights
That I can see at home today.

All My Senses

I can spy with my little eye
I can hear with my little ear
I can smell with my little nose
I can touch with my little toes
I can taste with my little tongue
Now all my senses I have sung.
All work well. X2

Design, Art and Modelling

Pencils and pens

- *Now you see it…:* Ask children to fold a piece of paper in half and while wearing a blindfold using a range of drawing media create a pattern on one half. Use touch and concentration to keep the drawing on the page! Then ask them to take off the blindfold and try to copy the same pattern using their eyes this time!

Paint and print

- *Sensational finger painting:* Add different textured materials to paint and ask children to use fingers to explore how they feel. Try sand, rice, glitter, and seeds.
- *Smelly paintings:* Add strong perfume or peppermint extract to the paint and encourage children to enjoy using their sense of smell as they paint.
- *Cornflour magic:* Put a mixture of cornflour and water onto a plastic tray or table top. Ask children to push their hands through the mixture and enjoy watching shapes form and disappear.
- *Touchy feely printing:* Make a collection of natural or manmade objects with different textures such as sponges, corks, fruit, shells, pine cones, plastic bricks and wheels, lids, etc. and print on different textured paper and cardboard.
- *Painting to music:* On an easel, ask children to paint a big picture as some music plays. Try using

different types of music and see if it affects the results. Does the music inspire a picture, mood or pattern?

Collage

- *Textured squares:* Invite children to choose different textured materials to create contrasting squares that they can feel such as corrugated cardboard, sand-paper, cellophane, silver foil, netting, wool, felt, bubble wrap, lace, and so on. Can they challenge each other to identify the materials by touch only i.e. while wearing a blindfold!

Modelling

- *Squidgy painting:* Fill a self-sealing sandwich or ziplock bag half-full with shaving foam and add some food colouring or coloured ink. Seal the bag and then squeeze, squidge and slide watching the foam change colour.

Clay and dough

- *Clay tiles:* Roll clay out to 5mm thick and cut out a square tile shape. Press different natural and manmade objects into the tile to create patterns. Leave clay to dry, paint with bright colours and varnish.

Famous Art

Prehistoric art - Lascaux cave paintings

Cave artists: Look at pictures of cave paintings discovered in France in 1940s. Roll out irregular shapes in clay and paint with different shades of grey paint to look like stone. Leave to dry and then using black, brown or red oil pastels draw prehistoric style pictures. Alternatively, try using textured paint made from sieved soil and sand mixed with lard and paint on paving stones outside.

Dance and Movement

Warm Up

Sitting quietly listen carefully. What sounds can you hear? A bird? A plane? A car? People chatting? Encourage children to tell each other what they heard and then to mime those same things.

Dance

Feely Dance

Cover a floor space in different textured materials, ensuring they are securely fastened. Some suggestions include bubble wrap, bathroom rugs, bath mats, fine sand paper or rolls of cotton wool. Choose some music and then dance on the different materials with bare feet.

Movement Games

Blind man's bluff

One child hunts for other children in a safe clear space whilst blind folded. Once the child finds another child they try to guess who they have captured without the use of their sight.

Scented flannels

Scent individual flannels using flavourings such as vanilla essence, mint essence and lavender. Place the flannels around a clear open space. Children imagine they are on a treasure hunt. You call out a scent for them to find. The aim of the game is to recover the correct scented flannel first. The more flannels and scents the better!

Cool Down

Sign a nursery rhyme

Research some simple nursery rhymes and their appropriate sign language. The internet is a good tool for research. Children will enjoy trying to copy your hand actions to match their favourite nursery rhymes.

Shapes

Drama and Role Play

Drama games

- *Make a shape:* Ask children to find a space in the room and dance to the music. When the music stops, call out a shape and ask the children to make that shape with their hands or body.
- *Circle warm up:* Stand in a circle and all hold hands. Swing arms in and out, step in and out, drop hands, stretch arms up high, sink down low, stretch arms out front, to your sides, behind, march on the spot, hold hands again and walk around to the right and then to the left, stand still and shake hands, arms, feet, legs etc.

Mime

- *Rollaball:* Sit in a circle and roll a ball to one child in the ring without speaking. Just use eye contact and use a nod of the head or a wink. Then they must do the same and choose somebody else in the circle and roll the ball.
- *Pass the shape prop:* Pass a 2D shape around the circle and ask the children to mime using it as something that shape, for instance, a circle could be a wheel, plate or frisbee; a square could be a window, bag, book, etc. Try with 3D shapes e.g. a sphere could be a ball, fruit etc.

Drama skills

- *Shape characters:* Create characters in the style of the Mr. Men series and make up stories about them. Mr. Circle is round, easy going, quick, happy. Miss Square is slow, solid and reliable. Mrs. Triangle is nervous, edgy and a bit prickly.

Role-play

A shapes workshop

Set up: A work bench, carpentry tools, scissors, glue, tape, wood, cardboard, boxes, tubes, different shaped templates, junk materials etc. Plans for different shaped items such as shaped greetings cards, shaped models, jewellery made of shapes, shape pictures, and so on.

Roles: Carpenters, designers, customers.

Stories: It is a busy time in the workshop with lots of orders for different items; a special model gets broken or lost; the carpenters run out of materials; a new worker gets all the shapes mixed up; there is a shape picture competition.

Stories, Songs and Rhymes

Stories

Elmer by David McKee
Give children lots of squares and access to lots of different materials to create a collage of Elmer.

The Blue Balloon by Mick Inkpen
Act out the story and use a blue balloon as a prop.

A Triangle for Adaora by Ifeoma Onyefulu
Act out Adaora's search for shapes in Africa.

Shape Train by Mel Astill
Use different shaped sponges to print trains and other shape pictures.

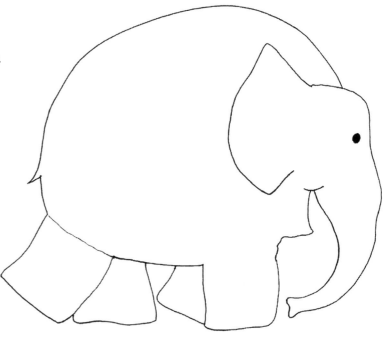

Shape Train

Jack's painting kept going wrong. He was feeling very cross. "Can I help?" asked his dad. "My brush won't paint a train with round wheels, square carriages and a pointy chimney" said Jack angrily.

"But you have to make your brush paint a train" explained dad.

Jack tried hard but it was no good. He felt sad. "Hmmmm.... I know what might help," said Dad mysteriously. He fetched a square sponge, a round sponge, rectangular and triangular sponges and a special piece of fluffy cotton wool.

Dad showed Jack how to print by dipping the sponges carefully in the paint and pushing them on to the paper. "Wow!" said Jack. He dipped the circular sponge in his black paint and printed six round wheels, he dipped the square sponge in his red paint and made two square carriages. Then he dipped the rectangular sponge in his blue paint and made an engine. Dad used the triangular sponge to make a pointy chimney.

Only the cotton wool was left, "Can you guess what that is for?" asked Dad.

"I can, I can," said Jack, happy with his shape train. "It's the steam that comes from the triangular chimney, on the rectangular engine, that pulls the square carriages with the round wheels!"

Songs and rhymes

(including circle games)
- My Hat it Has Three Corners
- Here We Go Round the Mulberry Bush
- Twinkle Twinkle Little Star
- Ring a Ring a Rosie
- Farmer's in His Den

I'm a Little Bubble
(Tune: I'm a Little Teapot)
I'm a little bubble, small and round
Floating up above the ground.
If you turn me over you will see
I'm still a circle, can't catch me!

A Triangle Has Three Corners
(Tune: My Hat It Has Three corners)
A triangle has three corners
Three sides it has as well
And if you play the triangle
It sounds just like a bell!

There Are Four Sides To A Square
(Tune: She'll Be Coming Round The Mountain)
There are four sides to a square, 1, 2, 3, 4,
There are four sides to a square, 1, 2, 3, 4,

There are four sides to a square,
And they measure all the same.
There are four sides to a square, 1, 2, 3, 4.

Make A Circle
(tune: Oh My Darling)
Make a circle,   X3
In the air.
Make a circle,   X3
Everywhere.

Design, Art and Modelling

Pencils and pens

- *Shape rubbing:* Secure some small plastic shapes on the table using blutack. Place a piece of thin white paper over the shapes and make rubbings using wax crayons.

Paint and print

- *Cork printing:* Cut corks both ways to create circles and rectangles. Ask children to use lots of different colours and print shape pictures. Try creating shaped people, vehicles and buildings.
- *Printing with pots:* Make a collection of different shaped empty plastic yoghurt pots and packaging. Press tops and bottoms into thin trays of paint and print line and solid shapes.

- *Symmetrical prints:* Fold paper in half and then open it out. Paint half a shape on one side so it touches the centre line. Fold the paper in half and press down to watch the rest of the shape emerge.

Collage

- *Sticky shapes:* Invite children to choose their favourite shape and using templates cut out as many different-sized versions out of a variety of materials. Stick these onto a piece of card to create a textured shape collage.

Modelling

- *Müller face puppets:* Use empty Müller yoghurt pots as moving puppets. Draw faces onto the larger section and add hair or hats. Practise moving the two parts together like a talking mouth.
- *Shape sorter:* Work together to paint a large square cardboard box a different colour on each face. Then cut a different shaped hole into each side and find smaller boxes to post through them.

Clay and dough

- *Clay coasters:* Use thinly rolled out clay to make round, square or triangle drink mats. Decorate with patterns using clay tools, leave to dry and then paint in bright colours. Add a piece of felt to the base to make them more stable.

Famous Art

Henri Matisse - The Snail

Shape snail: Use Matisse's collage as a starting point to discuss the shapes and pattern used to create the 'snail'. Ask children to make their own snail using prepared shapes or by cutting or tearing their own. Which other creatures could they make?

Dance and Movement

Warm Up

 Invite children to place themselves into a strange shape. Who can make the strangest, the longest or the smallest shape?

Dance

Balls galore

Provide children with as many different shaped balls as possible; footballs, rugby balls, tennis balls, ping pong balls, basket balls, squash balls and soft balls to name a few. Then in a clear open space allow children to dance with their balls expressing themselves freely. Choose some favourite music to accompany the dance.

Disco fever

Dance along to the classic disco tracks "D.I.S.C.O" and "Y.M.C.A" showing the children how to form the different letter shapes in the air.

Movement Games

Shape traffic

Look at the "Traffic Lights" activity in the Journey topic. Substitute red, amber and green with shapes. Call out a shape for the children to form with their bodies or hold up a visual picture of a shape.

Shape stop

Stick lots of different shapes to the floor. Play some favourite music. When the music is playing children dance about in their own unique way. When the music is stopped call out a shape. The children run to the shape called.

Cool Down

Provide children with either large chunky chalks or paintbrushes and water. In an outdoor space invite children to draw large shapes on the floor. (Adding glitter to water will ensure shapes last longer).

Shopping

Drama and Role Play

Drama games

- *I went to the supermarket:* This is a good game for concentration and listening skills. Each person adds to the list of items bought at the supermarket. See the topic of Food.
- *Who will buy?:* Choose four different shops and put up labels in each corner of the room: bakers, greengrocers, newsagents, chemists. Read out a shopping list and ask children to run to the correct shop to buy each item. Where would you buy apples, bread, magazines, oranges, medicine, cakes, toothpaste, sweets?

Mime

- *Which shop?:* Ask children to mime visiting different types of shops and buying appropriate items. Can the others guess which shop they are miming?

Drama skills

- *Five currant buns:* Act out the rhyme in different ways. Add drama by changing the type of buns or cakes, the prices, and the customers who come to the shop. Go behind the scenes and act out making the bread or cakes for the baker's shop.
- *Marketing:* Ask children to think of some news to share. Take turns interviewing each other using an echo microphone. Remember to speak into the microphone each time. Pretend to interview people who are shopping and talk about new products and offers. Create an advertisement for an exciting new product.

Role-play

Open a shop - supermarket, bakers, greengrocers

Set up: Uniforms, shelves, tables, purses, money, baskets, trolleys, cash till, bags. Suitable stock for each shop e.g. empty food boxes packed with newspaper and sealed; salt and flour dough cakes and biscuits; pretend bread; plastic fruit; fruit made from newspaper, modroc and paint.

Roles: Shopkeepers, shelf stackers, checkout staff, baker, greengrocer, customers, suppliers.

Stories: The shop runs out of items; impatient customers; a child is lost in the shop; lazy workers; customers complaining about broken biscuits or mouldy potatoes. A shopper forgets their shopping list; there is a power cut in the shop, the freezer packs up!

Stories, Songs and Rhymes

Stories

 The Shopping Basket by John Burningham
Act out the boy's encounters with different animals and make up new problems.

The Shopping Expedition by Allan Ahlberg
Use the beautiful artwork to inspire paintings of the adventures that can ensue when a simple shopping trip turns into an expedition!

My Granny Went to Market by Stella Blackstone
Add sound effects to the rhyme as granny goes around the world on a magic carpet shopping for treasures in all the places she visits.

The Shopping List by Judith Harries
Act out the story.

The Shopping List

Sam loved making lists in his head. He liked to list all of his toys, the names of his friends in Reception, all the people in his family, and even the names of as many cars as he could remember. Sam had an excellent memory.

Dad came in from work, tired and a bit grumpy. "Where is my magazine?" he asked. Sam remembered seeing it in the bathroom and so he told Dad.

Carys, Sam's sister was always losing her things. "Where is my diary?" she moaned. Sam remembered seeing it in the kitchen and so he told her.

Even at school, Sam liked to remind Miss Atkins where she had put things or what they were supposed to be doing each day! Gran used to say that Sam's head was full of lists.

One day, Sam went shopping with Gran. He liked going shopping. He liked the way everything was organised at the supermarket in rows, stacked neatly waiting to be chosen. As they walked up the fruit and veg aisle Gran stopped. "Oh dear, I've forgotten the shopping list again Sam", she said. Sam smiled. "Don't worry Gran", he said. "I bet I can remember everything we need from the list in my head." And he did, even his favourite orange lollipops!

Songs and rhymes

- Hippety Hop to the Corner Shop
- Five Currant Buns in the Baker's Shop
- Simple Simon

Let's Go Shopping in the Market
(Tune: She'll be Coming Round the Mountain)
Let's go shopping in the market for your tea, X2
Let's go shopping in the market, shopping in the market,
Shopping in the market for your tea.

We'll buy lots of fruit and veg, at every stall, X2
We'll buy lots of fruit and veg,

Lots of fruit and veg,
Lots of fruit and veg, at every stall.

At the Supermarket
(Tune: Sing a Song of Sixpence)
At the supermarket
Shopping with my mum
Helping push the trolley
Having lots of fun
Choosing lots of favourite
Things to drink and eat
If I'm good you never know
She may buy me a treat!

Design, Art and Modelling

Pencils and pens

- *Shopping lists:* Use strips of thin paper coiled into a till roll. Draw simple shapes of fruit, vegetables, tins, etc. on to the paper using felt pens and pencils. Who can make the longest shopping list?

Paint and print

- *Block prints:* Use foam trays from fruit and vegetables. Choose a smooth tray and trim off the edges to make a flat tile. Draw onto the plastic using a ball point pen. Apply printing ink/paints onto the tile using a roller. Press print repeated images onto a piece of paper.
- *Posters and adverts:* Look at adverts and posters for different shops and products. Design posters to advertise your favourite shops.

Collage

- *Trolley dash:* Make a simple trolley template (see templates at the back of this book) from thin card or stick half of a plastic shopping bag onto a piece of card. Cut out a range of pictures from catalogues. Use food magazines, supermarket leaflets, toy brochures, etc. Invite children to choose what to buy and stick their choices into the trolley.

Modelling

- *Junk modelling:* Use any food boxes and packaging to create fantastic models. Invite children to use their imagination freely to create any shape or object they choose.
- *Shopping bags:* Look at a collection of shopping/carrier bags. Make new bags from empty cereal boxes turned

inside out and painted with stripes, words, logos, etc. Reassemble the box and add handles using string, ribbon or card. Go shopping!

- *Market stall:* Make a model market stall using an upside down, empty shoebox. Add a frame and a canopy using lolly sticks, tubes, dowelling and a sheet of stripy paper. What will the stall sell? Make fruit, vegetables, fabrics, clothes, etc and glue onto the stall. Create a whole market square with lots of different stalls.

Clay and dough

- *Bakery goods:* Use salt and flour dough to make lots of different sorts of cakes, bread and biscuits to sell at the baker's shop. Try jam tarts using white and red dough, scones, and sausage rolls.

Famous Art

Andy Warhol – Campbell's Soup

Food packaging: Use labels from tins to create collages in the style of Warhol. Try repeated patterns and shapes.

 Dance and Movement

Warm Up

 Shopping List Rhyme
Act it out together with appropriate actions suggested by the children

Jelly on a plate x 2
Wibble Wobble Wibble Wobble Jelly on a plate
Sausage in a pan x 2
Sizzle sozzle x 2 Sausage in a pan
Curry in the pot x 2
Stir it up x 2 Curry in the pot
Chapattis in your hand x 2
Pat them here pat them there Chapattis in your hand

Can you create any more verses?

Dance

 This is the way we do our shopping
(perform to the tune of Here we go round the mulberry bush)

This is the way we walk to the shops
(walk around the room)
This is the way we push our trolley
(motion pushing trolley around the room)

This is the way we reach for our food
(stretch up to the shelves)
This is the way we pack our bags
(motion putting shopping into bags)

 One Child Went to Go
(perform to the tune of One man went to Mow)

One child went to go went to go shopping
One child and their basket went to go shopping
Two children went to go and so on.....

Start with one child and keep going until all the children have joined the shopping trip. Providing children with dressing up clothes and suitable props will further enhance the performance.

Movement Games

Checkout race
Children sort themselves into teams and sit in a line. They will pretend to be a checkout conveyor belt at the supermarket. At the beginning of each checkout place an equal number of shopping items. When the music starts the children pass each item down their line with each child calling out a beep sound as they pass the items. The first team to get all their shopping to the end of the checkout wins! Vary the game by having children repeating it standing, passing items over their heads or through their legs.

Shopping madness
Invite half the children to be shoppers and the other half to be the wind. The wind holds the edges of a parachute and moves it up and down in big motions. Scatter shopping items around the room. When you call out "go", the shoppers must try to get all the shopping items into the parachute before the wind can blow them out again. Repeat with children switching roles. Great Fun!

Cool Down

 Lie down on the floor on your backs with arms by your side and legs outstretched. Say the following rhyme;
Lifts going up
(Raise legs up slowly)
People going up
(raise arms slowly)
People getting out
(spread arms out wide)
Lifts going down
(lower legs to the floor slowly)

Once children are confident with the rhyme and actions, have different children call out the rhyme to the group.

Space

Drama games

- *Space conversations:* Sit in a circle and ask the children to make up some alien voices and sounds and take turns to have a 'space conversation'.

Mime

- *Moon walking:* Mime different space movements such as 'taking off' in which children crouch down, count down slowly and then jump into the air like a rocket; 'in orbit', children move round in circles slowly; 'space walk', children are astronauts floating in space connected to the rocket by a wire; 'touch down', slowly sink down onto the moon surface; 'moon walking', pretend to walk in a no gravity atmosphere with heavy moon boots.

Drama skills

- *Noises off:* Use different musical instruments and sounds to make strange sounds behind a screen. Ask the children to react and imagine what the sounds could be. Ask the children to improvise their own sounds. Make sure each situation is resolved safely i.e. the sounds turn out to have a perfectly reasonable explanation.
- *Group aliens:* Try some physical drama. In small groups, ask children to make an alien using their bodies and faces. They will need to decide how many legs, heads, and eyes their alien has! Can they create an alien language and have a conversation with another alien in the group? Organise a parade of aliens along to some spooky music such as 'Saturn' from Holst's Planet's Suite.

Role-play

A rocket landing on the surface of a planet or the moon

Set up: Use the climbing frame as a rocket. Alternatively, arrange some home corner furniture in a circle. Cover big tyres in fabric to make craters, hang black drapes for a space backdrop with silver or luminous stars and planets. Convert a sit-and-ride toy into a space buggy by covering it with aluminum foil. Space suits and helmets to dress up in. Oxygen tanks made from empty pop bottles.

Roles: Captain, navigator, astronauts, aliens.

Stories: First voyage to a new planet; meet some friendly or hostile aliens; the rocket breaks down; the astronauts get lost on their way home. Act out the story of *Whatever Next?* by Jill Murphy,

Stories

Whatever Next? by Jill Murphy
Act out the story using props such as a cardboard box, a colander, boots, an apple, biscuits, toy owl etc.

Bringing Down the Moon by Jonathan Emmett
Paint different sized moons using fluorescent paint and draw pictures of Mole trying to reach the moon in different ways.

The Way Back Home by Oliver Jeffers
Draw, or paint pictures or design model martians or aliens that the boy meets in space.

Beegu by Alexis Deacon
Create space pictures using white paint flicked onto black paper with a toothbrush. Cut out Beegu from yellow card, felt or fun fur and add him to the background.

Songs and rhymes

- Five little men in a flying saucer
- Aiken drum
- Twinkle twinkle little star

I Went to Visit the Moon
(Tune: I Went to Visit a Farm One Day)
I went to visit the moon one night!
I saw an alien, what a fright!

Choose the third line from these:
It was such a scary sight
Was it green or was it white?

Was it heavy or was it light?
Did it try to start a fight?
Did it scream or shout or bite?

Space is a Place

Space is a place
I'd like to go
Where nobody's been
And nobody's seen
And aliens play hide and seek.
Space is a place
I'd like to go
And look at the earth
The place of my birth
And all the other planets.
Space is a place
I'd like to go
To study the stars
To land on Mars
And disappear in a black hole.

Design, Art and Modelling

Pencils and pens

● *Scratch art:* Draw thick stripes of wax crayon on a sheet of paper or card. Remind children to press down hard so the colours are strong. Paint over the top with black poster paint or ink and allow to dry. Scratch off circle shaped planets and pointy stars to create a space picture.

Paint and print

● *Splatter painting:* Use metallic or luminous paint on black paper. Splatter with toothbrushes and pipettes for a space background. Add shooting stars, rockets, astronauts and planets cut from white or luminous sticky paper in the foreground.

Collage

● *Mighty Martians have arrived:* Use different collage materials to create a picture of a fantasy Martians from the planet Mars. Cut out the shapes and mount onto a planet surface background created using lots of hot colours – red, yellow, gold, orange, etc. Try using springs made from folded card or metal to mount the aliens so they wobble!

Modelling

● *Model planets:* Help children to blow up a balloon to make a spherical planet shape. Cover in two layers of papier mâché using flour and water glue and torn newspaper. Leave to dry, paint with bright colours and suspend from the ceiling.
● *Rocket man:* Use huge cardboard boxes from an electrical store to build a role-play rocket together. Cut a door and make conical roof. Use cereal boxes covered in paint, aluminum foil, plastic lids and lolly sticks as control panels.

Clay and dough

● *Model aliens:* Use dough or clay to create model space aliens. How many eyes, legs, arms, and feet will they have? How will they move? Are they friendly or scary?
● *Glitter dough:* Add glitter to some playdough and cut out stars and planets.

Famous Art

Georgia O'Keefe - Ladder to the Moon
What's in space?: Ask children to paint or cut and stick their own ladder on a pale blue background. Talk about what they will find at the top of their ladder? What will it be like on the moon? Paint pictures of imagined life in space

Dance and Movement

Warm Up

 Pretend to get dressed as an astronaut

(Sing to the tune of *Here we go round the mulberry bush*).

This is the way we put on our space suit
For our journey into space
This is the way we put on our moon boots...
This is the way we put on our helmet....

Encourage children to emphasise and exaggerate each movement.

Dance

 Perform with children a journey into space by performing the following actions:

- Get into the rocket – open the door, close the door, strap yourselves in
- Get ready for take off – count backwards from ten to zero, then blast off!
- Fly through space looking at all the things you pass – stars, satellites and planets
- Land on a chosen planet
- Explore, walking with slow bouncing giant steps
- Take the moon buggy for a drive
- Take photographs of the things we see
- Get back in the rocket and travel home

Playing a piece from Holst's Planets Suite as background music will encourage the children to match movements to music.

Movement Games

 NASA Says
Play as you would Simon Says – change Simon for NASA. NASA calls out the following instructions for children to copy:

"Space rockets" children stand with hands in a point above heads; "Spinning planets" children spin round; "Shooting stars" children perform star jumps; "Walking on the moon" children walk about with giant slow steps; "Asteroids" children crouch down low curled up like a ball.

Cool Down

Sit in a circle on the floor. Encourage the children to take a deep breath in. As they breathe out pretend to be blowing up a big planet like a balloon, moving arms in a circle to shape the planet. Repeat several times before lying on the floor on your backs. Pretend to look up into the night sky. What can you see? Raise hands slowly in the air and wriggle fingers like shimmering stars. Roll wrists round and round like spinning planets and wave arms slowly side to side for satellites and rockets passing by.

Spring

Drama games

- *Waking up:* Ask children to find a space in the room and curl up small and pretend to be asleep, hibernating over winter. Gradually narrate their 'waking up' for Spring by wiggling fingers, stretching arms, yawning, sitting up, standing, stretching and finally springing awake!
- *Wake up voices:* Use this echo game to wake up voices after a long winter sleep. Ask children to echo or copy every sound you make with your voice. Swoop from high to low, roar, squeak, hiss etc.

Mime

- *Spring animals antics:* See the topic of Animals. Concentrate on Spring animals such as rabbits hopping, frogs jumping, caterpillars crawling, lambs bouncing, birds flying, etc.
- *The very hungry caterpillar:* Mime the story of the caterpillar as he eats lots of different food and then changes into a pupa and finally a beautiful butterfly.

Drama activities

- *The magic egg:* Ask the children to work with a partner or small group to create a drama about time travel. Give each group a small shaky egg and explain that they are 'magic' and once shaken enable the children to travel backwards or forwards in time to another time and place. Help them to make up adventures and show the rest of the group.

Role-play

Spring cleaning the home corner

Set up: Home corner furniture; lots of cleaning equipment e.g. cloth dusters, feather dusters, polish, brooms, bowls of soapy water, sponges and cloths; aprons; washing up liquid and bowl to wash all the cups, saucers, bowls and plates; party decorations and fresh flowers.

Roles: Children, cleaners, families, visitors.

Stories: Preparing the house for a special celebration; somebody refuses to help clean the house; somebody keeps getting in the way; some marks and dirt just won't come off!

Stories

The Very Hungry Caterpillar by Eric Carle
Paint symmetrical butterflies using folded paper.

When Will It Be Spring? by Catherine Walters
Create two contrasting collage pictures of Alfie in both Winter and Spring.

Flowers and Showers: A Spring Counting Book by Rebecca Fjelland Davis
Use words and ideas from the book to create a counting rhyme about Spring.

Ten Seeds by Ruth Brown
Act out the story using ten children to be the ten seeds all suffering different fates!

Songs and rhymes

- Two little dicky birds

Spring Cleaning
(Tune: Aram-sam-sam)
A cobweb here, a cobweb there,
A sticky fingerprint, dirt everywhere.
A cobweb here, a cobweb there,
A sticky fingerprint, dirt everywhere.
Spring cleaning, spring cleaning.
A sticky fingerprint, dirt everywhere.
Spring cleaning, spring cleaning.
A sticky fingerprint, dirt everywhere.

Spring Time
(Tune: Flintstones)
Spring time,
In the Spring time,
There are flowers growing everywhere.
Spring time,
In the Spring time,

Breathing in the clean fresh air.
Spring time,
In the Spring time,
Blossoms blooming in all the trees.
Spring time,
In the Spring time,
Listen out for the birds and bees.

Spring Pairs

(Tune: Two little dicky birds)
A chicken and a rabbit
Were sitting on a hill.
One called Charlie,
One called Bill.
Fly away Charlie,
Hop away Bill,
Fly back Charlie,
Hop back Bill.

Two little frogs
Swimming in a pond.
One called Rufus,
One called Ron.
Jump away Rufus,
Jump away Ron.
Jump back Rufus,
Jump back Ron.

Toss the Tasty Pancake

(Tune: Hokey Cokey)
You put some flour in first
And then some eggs.
Add some milk
And mix it all about.
Pour the pancake batter
In the pan like this,
That's what it's all about.

Toss, toss the tasty pancake X3
Knees bend, arms stretch,
Toss it in the air!

Design, Art and Modelling

Pencils and pens

- *Field sketching:* Take the children outside with clipboards and paper or sketch books and draw any signs of Spring – flowers, ducklings, lambs, blossom on trees, and so on.

Paint and print

- *Spring still life:* Ask children to bring in flowers from outside or home, arrange in a vase and use pastels, chalks and paints to paint pictures. Add fruit and other natural objects to make different still life arrangements.
- *Fan flowers:* Use different-sized rectangles of cardboard to print fan shapes. Put the edge of the card into a tray of paint and then fan out on the paper to make each petal and leaf. Print stems using straight edges of card.

Collage

- *Seed collage:* Make a collection of seeds such as sesame, sunflower, pumpkin and poppy and some small dried beans. Spread glue onto paper in swirly shapes and sprinkle seeds and beans onto the glue. Brush off any excess and leave to dry.
- *Mosaic plant pots:* Cover small plastic or ceramic plant pots with white tile grouting or glue and stick on small buttons to create a mosaic effect.

Modelling

- *Junk Spring flowers:* Make daffodils from single eggbox cartons painted yellow or cake cases stuck onto a four petal pre-cut cardboard base. Make tulips from empty plastic film pots with four bright petal shapes stuck around the sides. Use short pieces of white art straws and yellow plastic lids to create daisies. Attach the flower heads to stems made from rolled newspaper painted green or pipe cleaners. Put flowers together into a bouquet.
- *Chinese blossom trees:* Stick and twist pipe cleaners into a ball of plasticine and make a tree shape. Fold tiny pieces of pink tissue round the branches to create blossom.

Clay and dough

- *Smelly flowers:* Provide some pink, yellow or red playdough and spray with a flowery perfume. Use flower shaped cutters and press beads and sequins into the centre.
- *Clay Easter eggs:* Roll and flatten a ball of clay or salt-flour dough into an egg shape. Use clay tools to decorate with repeated patterns. Dry and then paint stripes using fluorescent colours.

Famous Art

Vincent Van Gogh
– Flower Beds in Holland

Flower after flower: Use this image as a starting point to create flower beds. Fold a piece of paper into four or six parts and fill up with repeated flowers. Draw, paint or print flowers or use different collage materials.

Dance and Movement

Warm Up

Pretend to be an animal waking up from a long winter's hibernation. The children can choose what animal they would like to be. Begin asleep then slowly wake rubbing eyes and having a slow stretch – exaggerate each stretch as if the animal has very stiff limbs. Gradually get up and leave the winter bed going out into the world blinking at the first daylight before going off to explore the first signs of spring and forage for food. Encourage the children to create their own movements and story line.

Dance

The Birdie Song
Children love to dance along to this party classic found easily on children's party CDs or downloadable from the internet. The children will love this silly dance with its crazy actions!

Hot Cross Buns
Invite the children to act out this song. Encourage them to select suitable props from within the room to use for their performance.

Little Bo Peep
As above

Movement Games

Egg & Spoon
Give the children hard boiled eggs to decorate in any style they choose. Then hold a traditional egg & spoon race.

Duck Waddle
Children bend over and hold onto their ankles then race whilst quacking like a duck to a designated point.

Cool Down

May Day ribbons. A long ribbon tied to a stick or a long floaty scarf is ideal for this cool down activity. Show the children how they can move their ribbons with unhurried, controlled movements ensuring they have the opportunity to stretch their limbs. Make large circles in the air, wave the ribbon in long swaying motions above your head or move the ribbon up and down above your head and to the floor. Ensure the children have ample time to explore the ribbons for themselves.

Summer

Drama games

- *Take your voices for a walk:* Ask the children to change the pitch of their voices in response to some simple pictures (see diagrams).

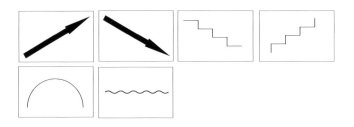

- Develop speaking voices by practising saying some summery tongue-twisters such as 'she sells sea shells on the sea shore', or 'Peter Piper picked a peck of pickled pepper'. Try these new ones: 'sing seaside songs in the season of summer' or 'nice icy ice creams and soft strawberry sundaes'. See the topic of Colours.

Mime

- *Feeling hot hot hot!:* Ask the children to mime walking through the desert, slowly stepping on the hot sand, getting slower and slower, dripping with sweat, needing a drink and collapsing onto the sand.

Drama skills

- Improvise a drama about a picnic in the park. Talk about the characters. Prepare the picnic by writing a list of food and then pretend to make the sandwiches and drinks and pack them into a picnic basket. Mime the journey to the park and set up a picnic spot. What could go wrong at the picnic? Someone could get lost, stung by a wasp, or the weather turn bad, dad remembers he has to go to work. What could go right?

Role-play

Ice cream van or stall

Set up: Convert a screen and chairs into a van, attach cardboard wheels to the side and add a striped awning. Make ice creams from cones of cardboard and tissue paper. Cash till, money, lolly wrappers, posters, price lists etc. Record a jingle for the ice cream van using a glockenspiel.

Roles: Ice cream seller, customers, other drivers.

Stories: There are no customers, too many customers; a rude ice cream man; the van runs out of everything, gets involved in car chase; a jingle gets stuck and won't stop.

Stories

Sports Day by Nick Butterworth
Write and sing a chant to perform at sports day to cheer on the children.

Dogger by Shirley Hughes
Produce a drama about losing a favourite toy and then finding it again.

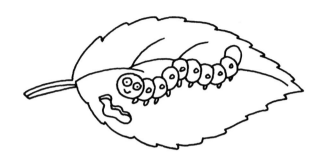

 The Winter King and the Summer Queen by Mary Lister
Create paintings that use colour and texture to
contrast winter with summer.

 We're Going On A Picnic by Pat Hutchins
Get children to plan and design their own picnic,
using their favourite food or drink.

Songs and rhymes

- The sun has got his hat on
- We're all going on a summer holiday

The Summer Fair

(Tune: The Animal Fair)
I went to the summer fair,
The sun shone everywhere.
The children played,
The parents stayed,
And everyone was there.
I went to lots of stalls,
Tombola, books and all
And then it rained, we all got wet,
And what became of the summer,
Summer, summer, summer…

It's A Picnic

(Tune: In the Navy)
It's a picnic
The sandwiches are made
It's a picnic
The picnic cloth is laid
It's a picnic
Let's drink some lemonade
It's a picnic
It's a picnic.

It's a picnic.
So come and join us too.
It's a picnic.
With treats for me and you.
It's a picnic.
A perfect summer view
It's a picnic.
It's a picnic.

Design, Art and Modelling

Pencils and pens

- *Spiral suns:* Choose sunshine colours and a large piece of circular paper. Make the pen travel round and round from the centre and repeat with other hot sunny shades until the sun is filled! Try using different types of lines – broken, dotty, spiky, wavy.

Paint and print

- *Fingerprint flowers:* Use finger paint or printing inkpads and make flower shapes using thumb and finger prints. Draw in stems and leaves with green pens.
- *Ice lolly painting:* Freeze water and food colouring into ice cube trays or ice lolly moulds. Add lolly or cocktail sticks before the ice sets hard. Use the coloured ice to paint cool pictures for a hot summer's day. Alternatively, try sprinkling dry powder paint onto the paper and then painting with plain water ice cubes.

Collage

- *Picnic time:* Draw round a template of a lunch box (see templates at the back of this book). Ask children to cut out pictures of tasty picnic food from magazines and stick onto the box.

Modelling

- *Palm trees:* Fringe the long side of a piece of newspaper. Roll up into a tube so the branches hang down like a palm tree. Secure with sticky tape. Paint trunks brown and leaves green. Make lots of trees and decorate the setting for summer.

Clay and dough

- *Clay sunflowers:* Roll out the clay to about 5mm thick. Cut out a flower shape using a cutter or blunt knife. Press sunflower seeds into the centre of the flower head and leave to dry.

Famous Art

Guiseppe Archimboldo – Summer (One of a set of four seasonal paintings!)

Summer faces: What is the Summer portrait made from? Which ripe summer fruits can the children see? Use magazine cut outs or fruit prints to create a summer face! What would make a good nose, ear or chin? Try using apples, lemons, starfruit, kiwis, etc.

Dance and Movement

Warm Up

As a group, form a circle standing up. Hold hands and move around in a circle as if you are the sun shining brightly. Stretch arms out in front and wriggle fingers, stretch arms behind and wriggle fingers, stretch arms in front and then down to the ground. Break away from the circle and encourage children to move around the room as individual suns shining in the sky.

Dance

Beach party

Set the room or outdoor space as a beach party; sandpits, paddling pools, beach balls, parasols and so on. Dress up in summer clothes and dance along to the children's favourite summer records.

Movement games

Hold a summer sports day. The children choose the games and events before setting up and participating.

Cool Down

Imagine you are the sun setting in the sky. If children wish to, give them the opportunity to perform individually in front of the rest of the group.

Toys

Drama games

- *Introductions:* Sit in a circle and take turns for each child to introduce themselves saying 'my name is _____, and my favourite toy is _____.' See the topics of Colours, Pets, and Weather.
- *Circular news:* Introduce a special toy to the children and explain that as it goes round the circle children can only speak when they are holding the toy. Invite them to share their news, thoughts and feelings. If a child is reluctant to speak suggest that they pass the toy onto the next child.

Mime

- *Rollaball:* See Shapes.
- *Toy parade:* Invite the children to move around the room like different toys such as marching toy soldiers, floppy rag dolls, racing cars, bumbling teddy bears, stiff bleeping robots, jumping jack-in-the-boxes, dancing dolls, trundling Daleks, and spinning tops.

Drama skills

- *Film a toy advert:* Choose a favourite toy, or design a new toy such as 'a chocolate button machine' or a 'robotic frog', and film an advertisement for it. Talk about why children will want this toy. What can it do that is new? How much will it cost? Ask children to pretend to be in the studio with cameras filming the advert. What might go wrong?
- *Toy Story:* Talk about the Toy Story films and act out favourite scenes such as the arrival of Buzz LightYear, moving house, and escaping from the toy collector.

Role-play

A toy shop

Set up: Tables and shelves full of toys. Sort the toys into dolls and soft toys, cars and moving toys, books and puzzles, and so on. Cash till, money, sales desk, price labels.

Roles: Manager, sales assistant, customers, different toys.

Stories: Choosing the best-selling toy for Christmas; the toys come to life at night; being the last doll left in the shop; nobody buying a particular sort of toy; a competition to name a toy and win it.

Stories

I Love You, Blue Kangaroo by E. C. Clark
As the toys build up in the bed sing this song to the tune of '*There Were Ten In The Bed*':
There were toys in the bed, and little Lily said
'Roll over, roll over'
So they all rolled over and one fell out!

The Velveteen Rabbit by Margery Williams
Improvise a dramatic story about toys coming to life when the children are not looking.

Old Bear Stories by Jane Hissey
Make a collage out of pictures of the different toys from the stories.

Dogger by Shirley Hughes
Create a wall-display of a toy stall with a toy designed, drawn and painted by each child.

Songs and rhymes

- Miss Polly Had A Dolly
- Jack In The Box Jumps Up
- I'm Forever Blowing Bubbles

Favourite Toy

In the toy box, hidden away,
Lies the tatty bear.
Smiling boy, burrows down,
Grabs without a care.
Pulls the treasure to the light
Shakes it in the air.
Laughs and jumps about the room.
His favourite toy is there!

Girls and Boys

(Tune: Girls and boys come out to play)
Girls and boys come out to play
With all their toys they start the day.
Play with a rope and play with a ball,
Play in the sandpit and that's not all.

Girls and boys stay in to play
With all their toys they start the day.
Play with a puzzle and play with a game
Play together and play the same.

The Toy Shop

(Tune: How Much Is That Doggie)
How much is that dolly in the window?
The one with the long yellow hair.
How much is that dolly in the window?
The one next to that teddy bear.

How much is that teddy in the window?
The one with the red spotty bow.
How much is that teddy in the window?
The one next to that blue yoyo.

How much is that yoyo in the window?
The one that that is shiny and new.
How much is that yoyo in the window?
Oh please can I have that too?

Design, Art and Modelling

Pencils and pens

- *Flick a book:* Use an empty exercise book, notepad or staple together lots of paper. Show children how to draw a series of pictures on the edge of each page changing it slightly each time, for instance a figure walking or a face changing from happy to angry. Flick the pages and watch the picture change.
- *Jigsaw rubbing:* Find a variety of jigsaw pieces made from wood and thick card. Arrange on the table, secure with Blutack and place paper over the top. Rub a wax crayon lengthways over the paper and see how the pieces appear. Alternatively, use jigsaw pieces as a stencil, draw around, colour in and cut out!

Paint and print

- *Construction prints:* Use any available construction toys such as lego, sticklebricks, duplo, mobilo, knex, etc. to print patterns and pictures. Can the children guess which toy has been used to make each picture?

- *Snap!:* Make a pack of snap cards. In groups, paint a series of simple pictures, flowers, shapes or patterns. Repeat until there is enough for a pack (4 each of six designs) allow to dry and play a game of 'snap' in pairs.

Collage

- *DIY jigsaws:* Ask children to choose a favourite greetings card or paint their own picture, laminate it and then cut into six to eight pieces like a jigsaw.

Modelling

- *Ball & cup:* Use a card tube, string, paper and one section of an egg box or empty film canister. Thread the string through a hole in the egg box or film pot and fix on to the end of the tube. Make a ball with scrunched paper and sticky tape – fix the other end of the string onto this. Can the children catch the ball in the cup?

Clay and dough

- *Skittle fun:* Use playdough or plasticine to make a set of eight mini skittles. In pairs, roll a plasticine ball, bouncy ball or marble and play!

Famous Art

Jane Hissey - Old Bear (series of books)

Big toys: Share a story about toys and observe the illustrations. What do the children think each toy would feel like to touch? Ask them to paint a big portrait of their favourite toy from the story.

Dance and Movement

Warm Up

This rhyme is great for warming up.

Jack in a box curled up small
(crouch down low with hands over heads)
Nobody knows he's there at all
(shake heads)
But if you suddenly lift the top
Up up up he pops
(jump up high with arms outstretched)

If possible give the children large cardboard boxes to jump up out of. It might be fun to have several jacks in one box.

Dance

Rag Dolls & Soldiers

Children choose to be either a rag doll or a soldier. Ask the rag dolls to have very floppy limp movements and the soldiers to have very rigid marching movements. You will need two pieces of music, one piece very gentle and gay whilst the other should be regimented and stern: "The Drummers Call" and "The Dance of the Sugar Plum Fairy" from The

Nutcracker are ideal. Explain to the children that when their music is playing they can move, but when it stops they must remain still and frozen. Switch between the two pieces of music to create the dance.

Choo Choo Train set

Children line up to play follow the leader with the child at the front elected as the driver. The driver could wear a flat cap or have a whistle. Children follow a chosen route – maybe a track drawn with chalk or marked out by cones. Once at the end a new driver is selected and the train returns back along the track. Allow the children to create the track they will follow. If you wanted accompanying music, the Thomas the Tank Engine theme tune is often popular.

Movement Games

Spinning tops

Similar to musical statues. Children spin around the room as music is played then stop still when the music stops.

Cool Down

Ask the children to form pairs. Explain that one child is going to be a plastic action figure and the other is going to place that action figure in different stances. It may be an idea to demonstrate the object of the activity first. After one child has had time being the action figure, invite the children to swap roles. All the motions should be calm and controlled.

Water

Drama games

- *Co-operation:* Put out enough mats so there is somewhere for everyone to sit. Explain that the mats are islands and that all the children are living on the islands surrounded by water. When you say 'action!' they must leave the island and go fishing. Each time you say 'home' they must return to the nearest island. Pretend that a big storm comes and one of the islands is flooded. Now they must co-operate and fit into less space. Continue until there is only one island for all of them to squash onto.

Mime

- Sit in a circle and ask for a volunteer to mime using water in different ways for the others to guess. Try drinking water, making tea, washing hands, taking a shower, washing up pots, cooking, swimming, rowing a boat, having a bath, cleaning vegetables, and keeping fish.

Drama activities

- *Row row row the boat:* Ask children to sit with a partner and sing and act out the well-known song 'Row the boat'. Try the crocodile version and row quicker.

  Make up new versions with different animals, for example:

  Row row row the boat,
  Gently round the lake,
  If you see a tiger,
  Don't forget to shake!

Role-play

Undersea world
Set up: Lots of blue mats, drapes and curtains, garden netting, green crepe paper and material weeds, plastic fish and water creatures, stones, shells and rocks to sit on. A treasure chest with treasure inside. A wreck of a boat made from cardboard boxes and tubes. Mermaid suits, deep sea diving equipment, oxygen tanks made from empty pop bottles, swimming costumes, masks, flippers.

Roles: Divers, mermaids, swimmers, fishes.

Stories: Searching for treasure; unfriendly mermaids causing trouble; a search party sent out for a lost diver; going fishing; catching a new type of fish or sea creature. Act out the story of *The Little Mermaid*.

Stories

 Mr Gumpy's Outing by John Burningham
Act out the story.

 The Rainbow Fish by Marcus Pfister
Use lots of colours and one sparkly scale to create a small collage of fish or one large fish.

 The Pig in the Pond by Martin Waddell
Use voices, body sounds and musical instruments to add sound effects to the story.

 Mrs Armitage and the Big Wave by Quentin Blake
Draw designs and plans for a new boat for Mrs Armitage.

Songs and rhymes

- Row Row Row The Boat
- 12345, Once I Caught a Fish Alive
- Five Little Ducks Went Swimming One Day
- A Sailor Went to Sea
- The Big Ship Sails on the Alley Alley Oh
- Jack and Jill Went Up the Hill
- My Bonnie Lies Over the Ocean

This Is The Way I Wash My Hands
(Tune: Here We Go Round The Mulberry Bush)
This is the way I wash my hands
Wash my hands, wash my hands.
This is the way I wash my hands
When I'm using water.
(Substitute face/feet/knees, etc.)

Sailing Boats

(Tune: My Bonnie Lies Over The Ocean)
I want to sail boats on the ocean
I want to sail boats on the sea
I want to sail boats on the river
And catch lots of fishes for tea.

I want to sail boats on the ocean
I want to sail boats on the sea
I want to sail boats on the river
And sail there with you and me.

Animals in the Water

Racoon in the river
Seal in the sea
Pig in the pond
That makes three.
Animals in the water
Lamb in the lake
Parrot in the pool
Make no mistake.
Octopus in the ocean
Whale in the well
Panda in the puddle
Who can tell?
Snake in the sink
Bear in the bath
Bee in the bottle
You're having a laugh!

Design, Art and Modelling

Pencils and pens

- *Felt pen washes:* Draw a picture using lots of felt pens, different colours and thicknesses. Brush on water to create a wash effect.

Paint and print

- *Bubble printing:* Put a mixture of water, paint and dishwashing soap into a deep plastic ice cream container. Invite children to blow (not suck!) through a straw until bubbles are bursting over the top. Place a piece of paper gently on top of the bubbles. Remove carefully and look at the bubble prints.
- *Dancing paint* Choose some clear containers, jugs, bowls, jars or an aquarium and fill with water. Drop food colouring into the water using pipettes or spoons and watch the colours dance around.

- *Water painting:* On a sunny day paint outside with water and a mixture of brushes. Try painting on the floor, slabs, walls, gates, etc. and watch as the sun dries up the art!

Collage

- *Clear springs:* Collect a variety of shiny and/or transparent papers: cellophane, cling film, foil, sweet wrappers. Cut and tear into long strips to make the cascades of a waterfall. Use rectangular card with slits cut across to hang the cascades from or hang on a metal coat hanger.

Modelling

- *Jiffybag fat fish:* Draw the shape of a fish on the outside of a jiffybag (see templates at the back of this book). Cut out the shape, staple around the edges and stuff the fish with padding. Paint on scales using metallic paint.
- *Japanese hanging fish:* Cut out two fish shapes from tracing paper. Stick on both fish lots of overlapping circles or scales made from scrap paper, magazines and shiny foil. Staple the two fishes together and attach tissue or crepe paper ribbons to the tail. Hang up so the 'koi' catch the breeze.
- *Bubble wrap jellyfish:* Cut out a circle from bubble wrap or a small aluminum foil dish and attach tissue paper or wool tentacles. Attach to a wire coathanger to make a mobile.

Stepping Stones to Creativity

Clay and dough

● *Something fishy:* Roll some clay out to 5mm thick and cut out a fish shape. Make scales using finger nails or clay tools. Add a button for an eye. Paint the fishy tiles and give as a gift.

Famous Art

Katsushika Hokusai - The Great Wave off Kanagawa

Pastel splash!: Create a copy of this giant wave image using dark blue paper and pastels. Rub, smudge, draw and drag the colours to make a splash!

Dance and Movement

Warm Up

Imagine gently rowing a boat down a river. As you row, see how far you can lean forwards and backwards. Maybe you are in a canoe and you must alternate your oar from one side to the other.

Dance

Under the sea
Invite the children to move about like sea creatures. Let them move freely creating their own ways to portray each animal.

● A wobbly jelly fish
● A slippery eel
● A sideways crab
● A gliding ray fish
● A graceful fish
● A blown-up puffer fish
● A shark with its dorsal fin sticking out of the water

Splashing fun
Using a bubble machine, allow the children to jump about catching bubbles. Play whale or dolphin music to create a feeling of the sea. On a warm day take this activity outside and add paddling pools for the children to jump about in.

Out to sea
Gather children around the edge of a parachute or large sheet. Pretend the parachute is the sea. Is the sea choppy or calm? Can you create a storm at sea? Invite children to dance and move about underneath, moving in time to the waves above.

Movement Games

The diving game
Underneath a parachute place objects from the sea e.g. a sponge, a shell, a piece of drift wood, a loafer, a toy starfish, a toy crab, etc.

Then chant

"Childs Name Childs Name dive under the sea
And bring back a .... for me"
The child called runs under the parachute and retrieves the object requested while the other children keep the parachute moving with the waves.

Alternatives;
Dive into the pond........
Dive into the lake.........

Crab Races
Create a starting line and a finishing line. Children place themselves on all fours with their tummies upwards, and then race each other to the finishing line. You could also create a course for the crabs to move through. Outdoors this is simply done by marking out a course on the ground in chalk.

Cool Down

Swaying sea weed - Pretend to be sea weed. Slowly stretch up tall reaching arms above your head, stretch further by standing on tip toes. Can you balance as you sway backwards and forwards gently in the calm water? Stretch arms out to the side and sway side to side. Bend down low and sway hands along the floor. Encourage the children to move in their own individual ways.

Weather

Drama and Role Play

Drama games

- *Introduction:* Sit in a circle and ask children to take turns to introduce themselves by saying 'my name is _____, and my favourite type of weather is _____'. See the activities in Colours, Pets, and Toys.
- *Rain dance:* Ask the children to find a space in the room. Kneel down and tap fingertips slowly on the floor to make 'pitter patter raindrops'. Tap feet quietly on the floor as the raindrops get more persistent. Stamp feet as the rain gets heavier. Jump up and down and splash into the puddles. Use some music that gets faster and louder to accompany the dance.

Mime

- *Weather Beans:* Invite children to mime different types of weather for example: for rain put up an umbrella; for fog move slowly as though not able to see; for snow shiver uncontrollably; for sunshine lie down and sunbathe; for wind whirl around; for ice bend into a spikey body shape; and for a storm stamp your feet and clap hands.

Drama skills

- *The Weather Forecast:* Set up the television studio with a camera crew and equipment. Make a camera from junk boxes and tubes and paint it black. Hang up a large map of the United Kingdom and make a set of weather symbols. Ask for volunteers to practise saying the weather forecast. Add drama such as a flood warning, strong winds or stormy weather coming.
- *Blown by the wind:* Ask children to go on a walk as you narrate the following instructions: go for a walk, carrying a coat over your shoulder; there is a slight breeze, that is getting stronger, put on your coat. As the wind gets stronger, fasten your coat and walk quicker. The wind is against you now so put up your collar or hood. A gale is blowing and walking is getting harder and harder. Each step is a major effort. And then you FREEZE!

Role-play

Campsite

Set up: Tent, sleeping bags, fold-up furniture, camping stove, cooking utensils, plates, cups, water containers, dressing-up clothes for different weathers.

Roles: Families, the campsite owner or farmer.

Stories: The tent is blown away by the wind or storm; too much sun; a stray dog on the campsite; burning all the food on the camping stove; the car running over the saucepans.

Stories, Songs and Rhymes

Stories

 After the Storm by Nick Butterworth
Use wax crayons and bark rubbing to create a giant fallen tree from the park.

 On The Same Day in March: A Tour of the World's Weather by Marilyn Singer
Build a mobile to show the world's weather using a balloon and papier mache to make a model globe. Then suspend from the mobile cut-out pictures of rain, snow and sun from different areas of the world.

 Snow Storm by Heather Amery and Stephen Cartwright
Act out the story.

 Alfie's Weather by Shirley Hughes
Choose a poem for each season and add sound effects using instruments.

Songs and rhymes

- Rain, Rain Go Away
- I Hear Thunder
- The Sun Has Got His Hat On
- Here We Go Round The Mulberry Bush

If It's Sunny And You Like It
(Tune: If You're Happy And You Know It)
If it's sunny and you like it,

Clap your hands.
If it's sunny and you like it,
Clap your hands,
If it's sunny and you like it,
And you really want to show it,
If it's sunny and you like it,
Clap your hands!

What's The Weather Today?

(Tune: Row, Row, Row Your Boat)
Sun, rain, wind or snow,
What's the weather today?
Look out of the window
And see what's on it's way.

Sun is shining high
That's the weather today.
No clouds in the sky.
Let's go out to play.

Rain is pouring down
That's the weather today.
Put on your boots and fasten your coat.
Let's go out to play.

I'll Be Using My Umbrella

(Tune: She'll Be Coming Round The Mountain)
I'll be using my umbrella in the rain
I'll be using my umbrella in the rain
I'll be using my umbrella, using my umbrella,
Using my umbrella in the rain.

I'll be wearing my sunglasses in the sun….

I'll be wearing my hat and gloves in the snow…

Design, Art and Modelling

Pencils and pens

- *Weather diary:* Design and draw some simple weather symbols. Use to write a diary of the week's weather.

Paint and print

- *Raining pictures:* Paint a picture of an outside scene using runny paint. Then drop water or rain onto the picture using pipettes. Hang up to dry on an easel and let the water drain off even more.
- *Rainbow colours:* Paint blobs of seven rainbow colours next to each other. Place a tube on the paint and then

roll it round in a curved semi circle shape. Watch the rainbow colours as they spread out.

Collage

- *Sparkling raindrops:* Cut out raindrop shapes (see templates at the back of this book) and cover with aluminum foil, sweet wrappers, gold and silver paint, and cellophane. Suspend from an open umbrella.

Modelling

- *Which hat shall I wear?:* Use different materials to create hats for teddy to wear in different weathers. Stick them onto pictures of teddy (see templates on pages 34 - 35) or try them on a toy teddy. Try plastic for the rain, wool for the cold and straw for the sun.

Clay and dough

- *Weather mobile:* Use salt and flour dough to make shapes of weather symbols. Cut a hole in the top of each symbol with a straw. Bake in a cool oven. Paint and suspend from a wire coat hanger.

Famous Art

William Turner - Snow Storm

Stormy weather: Rag roll a storm using grey, purple, blue, white, black, and yellow paint. Cut out a small boat shape from black card and stick on top.

Winter

Drama and Role Play

Drama games

- *Keeping warm:* Choose three or four different ways to keep warm: rub hands together, stamp feet, jump up and down, and blow on hands. Use different signals for the children to follow.

Mime

- *Jack Frost:* Ask children to move around room in a spikey way with elbows sticking out, fingers stretched and spikey, walking in zigzag shapes. Choose one child to be Jack Frost and go around the room touching the other children and freezing them into icy statues.
- *Winter weather:* Mime different types of winter weather for example mime snowflakes through spikey body shapes, for ice shiver, for snowballs curl up small, for a snow storm whirl around fast, for a snowman freeze in the shape of a snowman, and for a hot snowman sink to the floor in a puddle of water!

Drama activities

- Ask the children to work together in a group and mime making a snowman. First, put on lots of warm clothes and walk out in the snow. Roll the snow into huge balls and construct the snowman. Add buttons, eyes, nose, mouth, and clothes. How does the group feel when the sun comes out and the snowman melts?
- *Freeze frames:* Explain that you are going to show a significant moment from a rhyme or story such as Humpty Dumpty or The Snowman as a freeze frame. Practise 'frozen' positions such as running, climbing a tree, looking startled. Play action/freeze, as in the topics of Dinosaurs or Farms. Make the freeze frame like a still photograph. Ask the children to suggest what each character might be thinking.

Role-play

Winter café

Set up: Tables, chairs, a winter menu on a blackboard, utensils, kitchen equipment, uniforms, a fire, real and pretend food.

Make some winter soup and fresh bread to serve at the café. Hot chocolate, hot dogs and hot drinks.

Roles: Waiter, waitress, chef, customers.

Stories: Bad weather, staff and customers are snowed in so nobody can leave the café; a rude waitress; a waiter spills some soup on the customers; a competition for the best winter menu.

Stories, Songs and Rhymes

Stories

One Snowy Night by Nick Butterworth
Act out the arrival of each new animal as they come to Percy's hut for shelter from the storm.

The Snowman by Raymond Briggs
Devise a simple dance to go with the music of the Snowman.

The Snow Lambs by Debi Gliori
Use different colours and a variety of materials to create contrasting inside and outside pictures or scenes.

Bear Snores On by Karma Wilson
Act out the story.

Play 'Wake up Mrs. Bear'. Get children to sit in a circle with Mrs. Bear asleep in the centre. Give Mrs. Bear a 'treasure' such as a musical instrument or soft toy to guard. Can a volunteer creep to the centre and take the treasure without waking her?

Songs and rhymes

- The North Wind Doth Blow
- Here We Go Round The Mulberry Bush

Trying To Keep Warm
(Tune: Jelly On The Plate)
Shiver in the cold,
Shiver in the cold,
Shiver, shiver, shiver, shiver,
Shiver in the cold.

Trying to keep warm,
Trying to keep warm,
Rubbing hands together,
Trying to keep warm.

Shiver in the cold…

Trying to keep warm….
Stamping feet, stamping feet.
Trying to keep warm.

Keep Moving
(Tune: One Finger, One Thumb)
Four fingers, one thumb, keep moving X3
And put on your mittens today.
Five toes, one foot, keep moving X3
And put on your boots today.

Winter Blues
I'm so lonely and cold and it's all bad news X2
I'm gonna sing the winter blues.

Winter Ways
Winter ways
Freezing days
Evergreen trees
Knobbly knees
Starry night
Snowy white
Icy puddles
Warming huddles.

Design, Art and Modelling

Pencils and pens

- *Stick trees:* Use black pens and white paper to draw spiky winter trees on a snowy landscape.

Paint and print

- *Icicle drip painting:* Spread runny white or silver paint along the top of some black or blue cardboard. Hang the painting up and watch the icicles drip down the page.
- *Frosty prints:* Go outside with the children on a frosty morning, find a patch of frost and press gloved hands onto the frost to make hand prints. Try foot prints using shoes or boots with interesting soles. Photograph the results.

Collage

- *Paper snowflakes:* Cut circles from thin white paper or plastic bags and then fold in half and half again. Cut shapes out of the folds and the edges of the circle. Unfold to reveal a snowflake shape. Cover with glitter and hang on the windows.

Modelling

- *Indoor snowman* Work together to scrunch sheets of newspaper into one large ball for the body and a smaller ball for the head. Wrap round toilet roll and pva glue until the snowman is covered.
- *Frozen/melting scene:* Make a collection of natural winter objects such as holly and other evergreen leaves, berries, pine cones, sticks, stones, grass, etc. Arrange them in a plastic tray and then add some water and freeze until set. Observe the changes as the scene melts.
- *Snow storms:* Stick a Christmas cake decoration or small toy onto the inside of a small glass jar. Add some water and a few drops of glycerine, some desiccated coconut or glitter. Secure the lid and shake gently to watch the 'snowflakes' swirl around.

Clay and dough

- *Snowmen:* Make extreme white playdough using cornflour and build some indoor snowmen. Make a family of different-sized snowpeople!

Famous Art

Claude Monet – Winter on the Seine

Snow smudge: Use this winter masterpiece to discuss cold colours, the colours of the sky and the snow. Use pastel blues and whites on an off-white, black or blue paper. Smudge and blend a snowy scene. Draw in some buildings and then smudge the snow onto the roofs.

Dance and Movement

Warm Up

 Imagine you are on an ice rink elegantly skating along. Your movements should be slow, sliding and graceful. Encourage the children to make every movement controlled and exaggerated. More confident children may enjoy performing their routines in front of an audience. The Waltz makes perfect background music. To extend the activity invite children to attach paper plates to their feet as pretend skates aiding their actions to flow as if on the ice.

Dance

Here we go round the mulberry bush on a cold and frosty morning

This is the way we put on our coats......
This is the way we put on our scarves......
This is the way we put on our boots.......
This is the way we put on our gloves.......
Let the children come up with some actions to match the song as well.

Rockin' Robin

Similar to the Two by Two activity in the Number topic. Adapt to use rock and roll music and create some rock and roll movements to match – kicking of the legs, slapping the thighs and then clapping hands together, doing the "twist" and "mashed potato" moves.

I'm a little snowman
(to the tune of I'm a little tea pot)
I'm a little snowman
Short and fat
(motion a short person then hold hands out wide)
Here's my scarf
(motion winding a scarf around your neck)
Here's my hat
(Point to an imaginary hat)
When the snow is falling
(motion snow falling with your fingers)
Here me say

Come and build a snowman on a winter's day
(motion building a snowman)

Movement Games

Jack Frost game
Start by explaining to the children that the word freeze can describe weather and also the action of stopping still as if frozen. Ask the children to move freely dancing around the room to music – "Walking in the Air" from The Snowman is perfect. When the music stops they must freeze as if Jack Frost has visited. Repeat until the music comes to an end. This game can be extended by choosing one child to be the sun. When the children freeze they cannot move again until the sun has come over to them and warmed them up.

Cool Down

Santa's Sack
Give each child a bean bag, if you don't have enough bean bags you could roll up a pair of socks, this works just as well and the children find smelly socks hilarious! Tell the children the beanbag or sock is a present from Santa. Ask the children to copy your actions. Suggested actions:

- Can they balance the present on their head?
- Can they place it on one shoulder and lift their shoulder up and down, then try the other shoulder?
- Can they place it on one foot and balance it there?
- Can they sit down and pick up the present between their feet?

How many other movements can the children think to do with the present? Play quiet Christmas themed music while you play.

Suggested story books

- *Pumpkin Soup* by Helen Cooper (Corgi Childrens)
- *Rumble In The Jungle* by Giles Andreae (Orchard Books)
- *Rumpelstiltskin* Traditional (Ladybird Books)
- *Sharing Shell* by Julia Donaldson (Macmillan Children's Books)
- *Snow Storm* by Heather Amery and Stephen Cartwright (Usborne Publishing)
- *Snow White And The Seven Dwarfs* Traditional (Random House)
- *Sport's Day* by Nick Butterworth (Hodder Children's Books)
- *Squirrel Nutkin* by Beatrix Potter (Frederick Warne Publishers Ltd.)
- *Stone Soup* Traditional (Child's Play)
- *Tadpole's Promise* by Jeanne Willis (Andersen Press Ltd.)
- *Tell Me What It's Like To Be Big* by Joyce Dunbar (Corgi Childrens)
- *Ten Seeds* by Ruth Brown (Alfred A. Knopf)
- *That Pesky Rat* by Lauren Child (Orchard Books)
- *The Baby Who Wouldn't Go To Bed* by Helen Cooper (Doubleday)
- *The Bad-Tempered Ladybird* by Eric Carle (Puffin Books)
- *The Blue Balloon* by Mick Inkpen (Macmillan Children's Books)
- *The Cat Who Wanted To Go Home* by Jill Tomlinson (Egmont Books Ltd.)
- *The Dance Of The Dinosaurs* by Colin Hawkins (Picture Lions)
- *The Elves and The Shoemaker* Traditional (Ladybird Books)
- *The Enormous Turnip* Traditional (Ladybird Books)
- *The Firebird* Traditional (Tor Books)
- *The Gingerbread Man* Traditional (Ladybird Books)
- *The Global Garden* by Kate Petty (Eden Project Books)
- *The Gruffalo* by Julia Donaldson (Macmillan Children's Books)
- *The Leopard's Drum* by Jessica Souhami (Frances Lincoln Children's Books)
- *The Lighthouse Keeper's Breakfast* by Ronda Armitage (Scholastic)
- *The Lighthouse Keeper's Lunch* by Ronda Armitage (Scholastic)
- *The Little, Little House* by Jessica Souhami (Frances Lincoln Children's Books)
- *The Little Red Ant And The Great Big Crumb* by Shirley Climo (Houghton Mifflin)
- *The Little Red Hen* Traditional (Ladybird Books)
- *The Mixed-Up Chameleon* by Eric Carle (Puffin Books)
- *The Night Pirates* by Peter Harris (Egmont Books Ltd.)
- *The Owl Babies* by Martin Waddell (Walker Books Ltd.)
- *The Pig In The Pond* by Martin Waddell (Walker Books Ltd.)
- *The Princess And The Pea* Traditional (Puffin Books)
- *The Rainbow Fish* by Marcus Pfister (North - South Books)
- *The Shopping Basket* by John Burningham (Candlewick Pr)
- *The Shopping Expedition* by Allan Ahlberg (Walker Books Ltd.)
- *The Snail And The Whale* by Julia Donaldson (Macmillan Children's Books)
- *The Snow Lambs* by Debi Gliori (Scholastic Hippo)
- *The Snowman* by Raymond Briggs (Puffin Books)
- *The Three Little Pigs* Traditional (Ladybird Books)
- *The Three Little Wolves and The Big Bad Pig* by Eugene Trivizas (Egmont Books Ltd.)
- *The Tiger Who Came To Tea* by Judith Kerr (Harper Collins Children's Books)
- *The Tiny Seed* by Eric Carle (Puffin Books)
- *The Train Ride* by June Crebbin (Walker Books Ltd.)
- *The Ugly Duckling* Traditional (Orchard Books)
- *The Velveteen Rabbit* by Margery Williams (Egmont Books Ltd.)
- *The Very Hungry Caterpillar* by Eric Carle (Puffin Books)
- *The Way Back Home* by Oliver Jeffers (Harper Collins Children's Books)
- *The Winter King And The Summer Queen* by Mary Lister (Barefoot Books Ltd.)
- *The Wooden Dragon* by Joan Aiken (Red Fox)
- *This Is The Bear* by Sarah Hayes (Walker Books Ltd.)
- *Three Billy Goat's Gruff* Traditional (Ladybird Books)
- *Tim, Ted And The Pirates* by Ian Whybrow (Harper Collins Children's Books)
- *Tyrannosaurus Drip* by Julia Donaldson (Macmillan Children's Books)
- *We All Go Traveling By* by Sheena Roberts (Barefoot Books Ltd.)
- *We're Going On A Bear Hunt* by Michael Rosen (Walker Books Ltd.)
- *We're Going On A Picnic* by Pat Hutchins (Red Fox)
- *We've All Got Belly Buttons* by David Martin (Candlewick Press)
- *Whatever Next?* by Jill Murphy (Macmillan Children's Books)
- *When An Elephant Comes To School* by Jan Ormerod (Frances Lincoln Children's Books)
- *When Will It Be Spring?* by Catherine Walters (Little Tiger Press)
- *Where's My Teddy?* by Jez Alborough (Walker Books Ltd.)
- *Who Are You, Stripy Horse?* by Jim Helmore (Egmont Books Ltd.)
- *Who's Making That Smell/Noise?* by Philip Hawthorn (Usbourne Books)
- *Why Should I Recycle?* by Jen Green (Barron's Educational Series)
- *Yucketypoo* by Jilly Henderson-Long (Lollypop Publishing Ltd.)

Suggested songs and music

- "Can We Fix It?" on *Can We Fix It?* by Bob the Builder (BBC)
- "Carnival of the Animals" on *Camille Saint-Saens The Carnival of the Animals* Symphony No. 3 by The City of Birmingham Symphony Orchestra (CFP)
- "Chitty Chitty Bang Bang" on *Chitty Chitty Bang Bang: The Original Soundtrack* (Varese Sarabande)
- "Colours of the Wind" on *The Best Disney Album in the World....Ever!* by Various Artists (Virgin TV)
- "D.I.S.C.O" on *D.I.S.C.O* by Ottawan (Laserlight)
- "Dinosaur Music" on *Dinosaur Music* by Schott Staedt (Wergo)
- "Drummers Call" on *Drummers Call: America's Fife and Drum Tradition* by The Fifes and Drums of Colonial Williamsburg (Colonial Williamsburg Productions)
- "Fast Food Song" on *Fast Food Song* by The Fast Food Rockers (Sony)
- "Flight of the Bumble Bee" on *Rimsky-Korsakov Greatest Hits* by Zurab Sotkilava (Sony)
- "Harry and His Bucket of Dinosaurs" on *Milkshake: The Album* by Various Artists (GTV)
- "He's a Pirate" on *The Best Disney Album in the World.... Ever!* by Various Artists (Virgin TV)
- "Heigh-Ho" on T*he Best Disney Album in the World.... Ever!* by Various Artists (Virgin TV)
- "I Love You" on *Barney's Colourful World* by Barney (Hit Entertainment Ltd)
- "I've Got No Strings" on *My First Disney Album* by Various Artists (EMI)

- "In the Hall of the Mountain King" on *Peer Gynt* by Edvard Grieg (Phillips)
- "L'Autunno" on *The Four Seasons* by Vivaldi (Classic FM Full Works)
- "Mambo Number 5" on *Mambo Number 5* by Bob the Builder (BBC)
- "Saturday Night Fever" on *Saturday Night Fever: The Original Movie Sound Track* by Various Artists (Polydor)
- "Summer Holiday" on *Fourty Golden Great*s by Cliff Richard (EMI)
- "The Bare Necessities" on *The Best Disney Album in the World....Ever!* by Various Artists (Virgin TV)
- "The Birdie Song" on *Let's All Sing Like The Birdies Song* by The Tweets (PRT)
- "The Nutcracker" on *Tchaikovsky: Ballet Suites* (Classic FM Full works)
- "The Planets" on *Holst: The Planets* by St Pauls Suite (Resonance)
- "The Snowman" on *The Snowman* by Howard Blake (Sony Budget)
- "The Ugly Bug Ball" on *The Best Disney Album in the World...Ever!* by Various Artists (Virgin TV)
- "Thomas the Tank Engine" on *My Favourite TV Themes* by Various Artists (Pinnacle)
- "Under the Sea" on *The Best Disney Album in the World....Ever!* by Various Artists (Virgin TV)
- "Waltz No. 15. Lullaby" on *Baby Einstein: Lullaby Classics* by Baby Einstein Music Box Orchestra (Buena Vista)
- "Y.M.C.A" on *The Best of the Village People by The Village People* (Island / Mercury)
- "Yellow Submarine" on *The Beatles Yellow Submarine Songtrack* by The Beatles (Parlophone)
- "Yo, Ho!" *The Best Disney Album in the World....Ever!* by Various Artists (Virgin TV)

Stepping Stones to Creativity

Photocopiable templates

Below are some templates that can be used as a starting point for many of the art activities in this book. Each outline can be enlarged using a photocopier, then traced around on a piece of card and cut out to provide you with a range of handy templates.

Mask
(Animals and Ourselves)

Sheep
(Farms)

Diamond
(Flight and Shapes)

Bear
(Bears and Weather)

Flower
(Growth and Spring)

Suitcase
(Holidays and Summer)

Balloon
(Flight)

Photocopiable templates

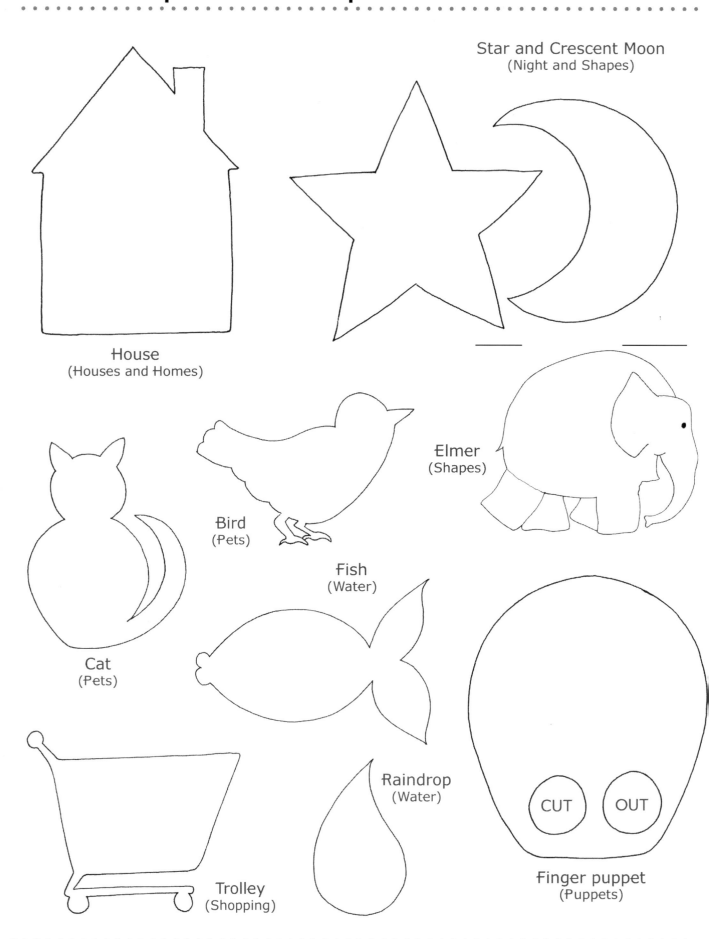

House
(Houses and Homes)

Star and Crescent Moon
(Night and Shapes)

Elmer
(Shapes)

Bird
(Pets)

Fish
(Water)

Cat
(Pets)

Raindrop
(Water)

CUT   OUT

Finger puppet
(Puppets)

Trolley
(Shopping)

Stepping Stones to Creativity